THE

BOOK

OF

KELLS

THE
BOOK ∴ ∴
OF
KELLS ∴ ∴

DESCRIBED BY

SIR EDWARD SULLIVAN, BART

WITH 24 COLOUR REPRODUCTIONS

FROM THE ORIGINAL PAGES

FOREWORD BY J. H. HOLDEN, ARCA

THE STUDIO PUBLICATIONS

LONDON & NEW YORK

First published 1914
Second edition 1920
Third edition 1925
Fourth edition 1933
Fifth edition 1952
Reprinted 1955

 Published in London by The Studio Limited, 66 Chandos Place WC2
and in New York by The Studio Publications Inc, 432 Fourth Avenue
Printed in Great Britain,
the text by W. & J. Mackay & Co Ltd, Chatham,
the plates by Edmund Evans Ltd, London

CONTENTS

PREFATORY NOTE

The Editor desires to acknowledge his indebtedness to the late Rev Dr Abbott, Librarian of Trinity College, Dublin, who kindly gave permission and every facility for the reproduction of the pages from the Book of Kells which appear in this volume. Special thanks are due to the Sub-Librarian, Mr Alfred de Burgh, whose invaluable assistance and untiring pains in revising the reproductions at various stages of the work reduced very considerably the difficulties with which the engravers were faced. As mentioned by the late Sir Edward Sullivan towards the end of his Introduction, the compound letters shown in the last five plates are from remarkably clever copies made by the late Mrs John R. d'Olier. Her son, the late Mr Isaac d'Olier, kindly placed the copies at the disposal of the Editor for reproduction in the present volume.

To those who have not examined the Book of Kells two features in the plates may require explanation, viz, the cut margins, which in some cases have damaged the designs; and the variation in the tones of the backgrounds. Both these defects are present in the original Manuscript. The first, as explained on page 23 is due to the ignorance of some incompetent binder to whom the priceless volume was entrusted about one hundred and forty years ago; and the second is caused by discoloration, for which age and the fact that the manuscript was for some time buried under the soil are probably responsible.

vi

FOREWORD

by J. H. HOLDEN ARCA

Principal, Wolverhampton College of Art

The Book of Kells is one of those documents which have fascinated generations of artists in every branch of artistic activity. Any modern artist or craftsman may study this book with the greatest pleasure and profit. Yet he may be quite unable to say just what it is about the Book of Kells which is the secret of its compelling interest. The Celtic and Early Medieval manuscripts, with their special significance and the social conditions under which they were produced, seem very remote from the life of to-day, and the Book of Kells is, in addition, so different in its presentation from contemporary calligraphy or indeed from any other kind of lettering, that a point of contact is difficult to establish.

One could instance similarities between the Book of Kells and paintings which have been produced in the last half-century, similarities such as interesting colour, unconventional conception of pattern, rhythmical basis of design and fantastic imagery; but all these are, I think, superficial likenesses. Really the Manuscript is as unfamiliar in feeling as the work of the Indians, the Chinese, the Incas, or the Peruvians. Probably it is because we are intellectually more familiar with conditions in Celtic Britain and Ireland than with, for example, the strange social life of China, that we seem to have a vague sense of familiarity with the Book of Kells; but artistically and spiritually it is just as far removed from us.

Why then, in this century which has seen the revolt against authority, the disregard of veneration for that which is old, and the emphasis on the present to the detriment of the past, does this remarkable manuscript retain its appeal? Surely it must be because of some intrinsic quality of the work itself, which, being above personal taste, has a value for each and every generation of craftsman, and which, in this epoch no less than formerly, will continue to lure the contemporary craftsman to seek the treasures contained in its pages and to become in his turn fascinated, instructed and absorbed. Now, if for a moment we think of the craftsman in relation to his craft (and for our present consideration I suggest particularly the calligrapher and the typographer) we see that he has, in every past age, felt compelled to develop and nurture within himself by observation, study and experiment, just those superb and excellent qualities which we cannot fail to recognize with pleasure and humility in the Book of Kells. They are qualities which the true student knows his craft intrinsically demands from him. Thus it will be in striving to acquire exquisite sensitivity, to develop a disciplined sense of rhythm, to cultivate the faculty of artistic discernment, that he will have this compelling interest in the Book of Kells.

For although vital writing and printing of all kinds depends ultimately upon the artist's sense of freedom and his opportunity to exercise his imaginative talents, his research must be very wide. It must include not only manuscripts and books from all countries and periods and all kinds of carved and engraved letters (especially those which are generally acknowledged to be perfect examples), but should extend far beyond the study of lettering, writing and illumination or typography, to embrace the great paintings and sculpture, fine pottery, silver and enamels. Only by such a broad study as this can the writer or printer develop impeccable taste. For the same reasons, careful familiarity with a great work such as the manuscript contained in the following pages, cannot fail to be a source of inspiration to potters, silversmiths, stained-glass artists and many others who will benefit by broad study and find in it a fountain of stimulating ideas. The rich, varied, almost daring colours are unified and harmonious. The lively and convincing use of the conventional idiom contrives to avoid monotony even in such a seemingly wearisome repetition as a genealogical table. The cleverly contrasted pattern forms, at times formal and geometric, at other times free and loosely woven, are united to form a well-balanced structure in which the large and small shapes are perfectly related so that each takes its right place in the economy of the whole.

The calligrapher will notice particularly the infinite variety of pen and brush strokes and the consummate technical skill with which the exact weight of each has been judged so that the ultimate result is a composition of great artistic beauty.

I welcome the reprinting of this publication which I regard both as a valuable contribution towards the maintenance of high traditional artistic standards, and as an example of undeniably superb craftsmanship.

INTRODUCTION TO THE
THIRD EDITION

Since the first and second editions of this consideration of *The Book of Kells* were written, some important publications have made their appearance the contents of which would seem to call for something more than a passing notice. Chief, and most recently published, amongst them, is Dr J. Bröndsted's *Early English Ornaments*, London and Copenhagen, 1924. Mr Reginald A. Smith, of the British Museum, in his Preface to the translated edition, expresses, in generous terms, his opinion of the value of the work in view of the close relationship between all branches of the Teutonic world during the period treated of. The work purports to be an attempt, not hitherto made, 'to give a comprehensive account of the origin and development of art in England in the 400 years which lie between the introduction of Christianity and the Conquest, with this limitation, however, that two domains of the art practice of the period, the figure art and interlaced designs, are left out.'

Anyone can readily understand the reason for these particular omissions who has had an opportunity of making himself acquainted with the monumental work of Professor Baldwin Brown, *The Arts in Early England*, London, 1903–1921, a series of volumes which completely cover all that need be said or illustrated in the domain of interlaced art. I shall refer later on to some extremely interesting observations arising from a new comparison between the art of the Book of Kells and that of its great rival, the Book of Lindisfarne, which forms part of the concluding volume of the series.

Dr Bröndsted's work, in so far as it relates to the vine-pattern design, its origin, development and general adoption in the British Isles, whether in monumental carvings or in illuminated manuscripts, is undoubtedly the result of extended research and close observation. If anything, it is possibly overdone so far as that particular form of embellishment became a feature of manuscript illumination— for, although it undoubtedly held a prominent position as a decorative distinction on the crosses of this country, it was by no means equally prominent in the illuminations of manuscripts. For instance, Bröndsted is found to say (page 85): 'Finally, in Irish art regions, we find the vine of north England both with and without animals in the Book of Kells (see Fig. 71), a fact which is not without its bearing on the question of the date of the ornamentation of the north of England.' But when we come to examine his own illustration of the figure referred to we find that it does not represent the vine pattern at all, the foliage, so far as it can be called so, being the very conventionalized trefoil which is so frequently found interwoven with the Kells forms of decoration. Dr Bröndsted seems, at times, too satisfied that the decorative features of monumental crosses moved *pari passu* with the embellishments of the illuminations: 'It can only be due to the chances of survival that the north English ornament is in our days to be found practically exclusively upon the crosses. The rest of the art and art industry in the north of England at the time must naturally have had a corresponding aspect and have worked with similar decorative material'. This is, to my mind, a belittlement of the extraordinary artistic range of which the Irish school of illuminators were pre-eminently possessed; and it must have been because of some such similar fancy that Dr Bröndsted, in another place, has had to assume—when he cannot prove—that the sculptured figures on the well-known Bewcastle and Ruthwell crosses are the outcome of imported foreign colonists: 'That these advanced and admirably executed sculptures, dated from shortly after A.D. 700, should be the work of native Anglo-Saxon stone-carvers, I consider absolutely out of the question, and what has been alleged in support of this view, most recently by Baldwin Brown, is, in my opinion, irrelevant.'[1]

Again, on page 35: 'A colony of Oriental artists, called in by ecclesiastics, may, in the course of the latter part of the seventh century, have established themselves in the north of England; the colony founded a school, and its mode of ornamentation was adopted by Anglo-Saxons and practised by them through a century and a half with constant modifications and conventionalization.'

As regards the vexed question of the approximate date of the Book of Kells, several arguments were advanced by me—some of them entirely new—in my earlier prefaces. I can find but few suggestions in Dr Brondsted's work which throw anything that can be called light on this very interesting topic, one in every way worthy of his admittedly rare powers of research and investigation. Having stated that the Kells Manuscript is, by the latest researches, generally placed early in the eighth century (page 71), he is content to add, in a note, the names of some of those who hold that view (with references to their works) and goes on:

[1] Professor Baldwin Brown's argument *contra*, with which I am in complete accord, will be found, in *The Arts in Early England op. cit.*, volume V, pages 287—89 and 306—13.

'Sullivan, *The Book of Kells* (Studio 1914) pages 29–39[1] keeps still to the old untenable position that the manuscript is necessarily dated IX–X by its leaf ornamentation.' The mighty Homer must, indeed, have been having 'a goodly nap' when he penned so misleading and unfounded a statement. The 'leaf ornamentation' is a very trivial point in connexion with my argument, which runs (as mentioned in the note) to many pages. Again, when he attributes to me a suggestion that I ever mentioned the *tenth century* as a possible date for the Kells Manuscript, he is merely dreaming of something which he had not read. The argument I brought forward (and for the first time) based upon the square or rectangular punctuation which distinguished the Kells volume from any other more or less contemporary manuscript of which I am aware, was one to which one might reasonably look for some scholarly reply from any careful student of early Irish palæography. Other grounds on which I based my views were connected with (a) the unfinished portions of the manuscript, (b) the contraction marks employed in the Latin text, and (c) the robe ornamentation of triangular groups of dots so frequently made use of. The dismissal of all these by the mere word 'untenable' can hardly be looked on as anything but uncritical—so much so, indeed, as to leave a reader somewhat doubtful as to the value of a good many of the author's other theories. To take the matter of the square-shaped punctuation prints alone, I have made considerable searches amongst the works of well-known palæographers, and up to the present have to confess with some surprise that I cannot find even one of them who has a word to say on that special shape, which is one of the prominent distinguishing features of the system of punctuation made use of in the Book of Kells. I had examined some original manuscripts and many of the reproductions which were available before writing my introduction to that Manuscript, and my conclusion then was that the square punctuation form was practically unknown in Latin script before the beginning of the tenth century, with the solitary exception of the Book of Kells. Recent further researches have only confirmed my opinion as to the late introduction of the square type of pointing, and also with regard to its value and importance in connexion with the date of the Manuscript itself. I have found no cases where the square type is employed before the eighth century. In the tenth century one begins to see traces of its use, for instance, the Cædmon manuscript,[2] A.D. 1000, which I had an opportunity of examining at the Bodleian Library last year, does contain some examples of square punctuation; while the *Encyclopædia Britannica*,[3] 1911,

1 This edition, page 41 *et seq*.
2 Now reproduced in facsimile, with introduction, by Sir Israel Gollancz, 1927.
3 Volume XX, page 577.

gives some lines of 'particularly fine writers of the twelfth century' from *Leviticus*, A.D. 1176, where, if the reproduction is to be relied on, there are in one line alone three distinct examples of the square-shaped pointing. In all the circumstances I am forced to the conclusion that the Book of Kells must be considered a *post* eighth century production until some manuscript of an earlier date is found in which the punctuation marks are distinguished by the square form so obvious in the Kells volume.

By universal acknowledgment, the two finest examples of Irish or Hiberno-Saxon illumination are the Book of Kells and its only rival, the Book of Lindisfarne. A comparison between the details of these two volumes is, naturally, full of interest to a student of the Kells Manuscript, more particularly when we remember that no one knows with any certainty which of them was the earliest to see the light. Professor Baldwin Brown has written some highly instructive pages on this comparison to which readers may be referred with every confidence.[1] A serious preliminary question between the two MSS is based on the strong divergence of opinion that exists amongst the chief authorities as to whether or not the Book of Lindisfarne is the outcome of the Northumbrian school of illumination or the work of a purely Irish artist. The matter is too deep and complicated for discussion here, and one can only say that of the latest writers on the subject Professor Baldwin Brown is altogether in favour of pronouncing the Lindisfarne an Anglo-Saxon work, while Dr Bröndsted[2] is equally emphatic in declaring it to be 'a purely Irish work in its ornamentation.' Professor Brown undoubtedly goes into the question at much greater length than his opponent. His opponent, too, praises the manner in which the differences in style between the two famous Irish MSS are set out, but adds: 'I see nothing in that difference which entitles us to call the Book of Lindisfarne Northumbrian . . . The whole animal and line ornamentation in the Book of Lindisfarne is as truly and characteristically Irish as anything can be; the difference between its illumination and that in the Book of Kells rests singly and solely on the difference between two individual ways of aesthetic feeling.'

One of Professor Baldwin Brown's arguments in favour of a Northumbrian provenance is thus expressed: 'In one detail also we distinguish an Anglian trait, and this is in the delight in the bird form which is far more in evidence in the Durham book than in the Kells or other Hibernian manuscripts. The creature, we have seen, is a cormorant, and cormorants breed on the Farn Islands . . . There

1 *The Arts in Early England, op. cit.*, volume V, chapters XV and XVI.
2 *Early English Ornaments, op. cit.*, page 92.

xii

is nothing improbable in the idea that the birds so loved of the Northumbrian designer are the sea fowl of his own Lindisfarne. . . .'[1]

In tracing the actual origins of both animal and floreated forms of ornament, an immensity of industry has been devoted to the subject generally, as well as to the multifarious forms into which such embellishments have shaped themselves both in monumental and illuminative art, in different countries and changing periods of time. Interesting as such researches may be to those who are absorbed in their pursuit, the results tend largely to a bewildering confusion where even the searcher not infrequently finds himself in a maze of contradiction from which a satisfactory exit becomes well-nigh impossible. Professor Baldwin Brown has some excellent and common-sense observations on the point with which I am in complete agreement. 'All through history', he says,[2] 'the designer of good ornament has worked on a basis of convention and has depended far less on copying from nature and on symbolism than literary critics imagine. . . . This is not the way the ornamentalist works. The forms he uses are as a rule derived from tradition, though they may be modified and enriched by the action of his individual taste and fancy as well as at times by details borrowed freshly from nature. The general scheme in the foliage panels on the crosses is the long established one of the undulating scroll, originating it seems in the Mycenaean period, in which the main stem gives out offshoots alternately to right and left that intersect the spaces with their curves and terminate in leaves, flowers, or branches of berries or fruit . . . not copied directly from nature nor selected for any reason of symbolism. The main scheme, on the other hand, is reminiscent of a symbolical motive. It is based on the vine, a floral motive that comes into vogue in the Hellenistic period and that was taken over with avidity by the early Christians with whom it carried a symbolical significance as the True Vine, the birds and animals feeding upon the grapes having a far-off reference to the faithful nourished on divine food.'

The following observations from the pen of a well-known palæographer are well worth bearing in mind when endeavouring to trace the origin of any particular form of design incorporated by Celtic artists in either illumination, sculpture or bronze:

'The great difficulty in understanding the evolution of Celtic art lies in the fact that although the Celts never seem to have invented any new ideas, they professed an extraordinary aptitude for picking up ideas from the different people with whom war or commerce brought them into contact. And once the Celt had borrowed an

1 *The Arts in Early England, op. cit.*, volume V, page 376.
2 *Op. cit.*, volume V, page 273.

idea from his neighbour, he was able to give it such a strong Celtic tinge that it soon became something so different from what it was originally as to be almost unrecognizable.'[1]

I have drawn attention in an earlier preface to a very remarkable use made of the triangular groups of red dots which are so frequently employed in the Book of Kells for the embellishment of the robes of holy persons. I find now that there are some few examples of a similar practice to be found in the Gospels of Mac Durnan (at Lambeth) and that Westwood[2] gives its date as 'not later than the beginning of the eighth century' although Dr Todd had dated the manuscript as of the century before. The portrait of St John in this Mac Durnan manuscript shows clearly the triangular groups of red dots both on the robes of the Saint as well as being used for general purposes of decoration.

Another Irish manuscript should be mentioned here, the Latin Psalter in St John's College, Cambridge, which Westwood dated eighth or ninth century. It contains a most weird illustration of the Crucifixion, 'unquestionably the most ancient specimen of Irish pictorial composition which has hitherto been given to the public. . . . The extraordinary propensity of the Irish School for marginal rows of red dots . . . will be evident from the drawing of the Saviour's habiliments, eyes, ears, etc.'

Strange to say the dots here are only marginal, and do not appear on the robes.

One cannot, therefore, without further evidence, rely very strongly on the dotted robes in the Book of Kells as indicating any special or traditional practice—a view to which I was formerly inclined—and as the only other instance I have observed of what I may call the Kells use of dots for the decoration of robes is of a later date and in no way connected with holy persons,[3] it must be the task of some other inquirer to discover what is the real meaning of the practice which is undoubtedly well established in the Kells manuscript.

Both Bröndsted and Baldwin Brown have a good deal to say concerning the arrival of scholars from foreign places into Ireland in very early Christian days. A good summary of the history of that important movement is to be found in quite a recent work, from which I take the following extract.[4]

1 J. Romilly Allen, *Celtic Art in Pagan and Christian Times*, London, 1904.

2 *Palæographia Sacra Pictoria*.

3 See Baldwin Brown *op. cit.* III, 374, plate LXXII (No. 1) representing an officer of the Court of Charles the Bald in which both sleeve and tunic are adorned with triangular group of dots (about A.D. 840).

4 Helen Waddell, *The Wandering Scholars*, 1927.

'Many extravagant things have been written about the Irish Golden Age: but in the sober scholar's prose of Bede, the story is miraculous enough. That fierce and restless quality, which had made the pagan Irish the terror of western Europe, seems to have emptied itself into the love of learning and the love of God: and it is the peculiar distinction of Irish medieval scholarship and the salvation of literature in Europe that the one in no way conflicted with the other . . . '[1]

Zimmer[2] has a theory that Ireland, secure from invasion in the shelter of the Four Seas, had long been a refuge of the timid scholars of Gaul, driven like thistle-down before the barbarian blast, and that even in the fifth century the Irish schools were notable. There is support for it in a casual reference by Columbanus to the judgment of Irish scholars in the fifth century on Victorinus of Aquitaine, the philosopher.[3] At any rate, by the sixth century the Irish schools were the most famous in Europe. The scholars came by the old trade routes, the three days' journey from the Loire to Cork[4]—in 550 a ship-load of fifty landed there—or up the Irish Sea to Bangor. That such a one 'forsaking his own country sojourned in Ireland for the love of God and of learning' becomes a commonplace of biography. Bede, writing of the great plague of 664, speaks of its ravages among the scholars: 'many of the nobles of the English nation and lesser men who also had set out thither, forsaking their native island either for the grace of sacred learning or a more austere life. And some of them indeed soon dedicated themselves faithfully to the monastic life, others rejoiced rather to give themselves to learning, going about from one master's cell to another. All these the Irish willingly received, and saw to it to supply them with food day by day without cost, and books for their studies, and teaching, free of charge.'[5]

EDWARD SULLIVAN, 1925

---

1 Poole, *Illustrations of Mediæval Thought*, page 10, *et seq.*
2 Zimmer, *Glossæ Hibernicæ*, 1881, and *The Irish Element in Mediæval Culture* (translated), 1891.
3 *Epist.*, i Migne, LXXX, c., 261.
4 Bröndsted, so far as my recollection goes, does not mention this approach to Ireland.
5 Bede, *Hist. Eccles*, iii, 27.

INTRODUCTION TO THE

SECOND EDITION

The success which has attended the publication of this work is, for two reasons, a source of much satisfaction to those responsible for the original issue of the book. In the first place, it amply justifies the belief, entertained by the producers when the work was brought out, that the presentation of a series of the unrivalled illuminated pages of the Book of Kells, in their actual colours, would be regarded as a welcome supplement to such previously published works on the same subject as contained only uncoloured representations; and secondly, it establishes the fact that there are many more persons—outside the world of connoisseurs, archæologists and palæographers— who are interested in the Manuscript itself, its history, and its artistic details, than was popularly believed to be the case. Since the date of the first issue, some six years of war and the turmoil that follows war apparently put an end to all serious investigations in the domain of Celtic palæography. No new light, so far as I am aware, has been thrown during those years on any disputed questions relating to the Book of Kells. Consequently there is little to add, from the studies of others, to the description of the Manuscript as given in the first edition. The Manuscript itself is, however, so full of information from within, that a slight study of even the reproductions given in this volume enables a careful observer to discover features of interest, previously unnoticed, on almost every page. Amongst such discoveries, made by myself, are a few perhaps worth mention.

I suggested in 1914 that the square-shaped punctuation marks, which are a characteristic of the Manuscript, might have some bearing on the vexed question of its date. What I have since noticed has considerably strengthened my original surmise. For instance, in plate x (lines 2 and 7) will be seen examples of the three-dot full stop which is frequently used to end a sentence throughout the work. It will be noticed, however, that in close and somewhat puzzling proximity to these stops there are other very similar dot-formed groups, actually on the line of the text, which, at first sight, might easily be taken for punctuation signs. They are in reality only ornaments; and the dots are in every case *round* in form, whereas the true punctuation marks are always rectangular. The fact that these two very similar forms are used on the same page, in conditions calculated to mislead a reader accustomed to the round forms of an earlier date, would seem to show that the Manuscript must have been written at a time when the transition stage was already past, and the square punctuation had definitely superseded the rounded form.

Besides this, there is another piece of internal evidence, as yet unnoted, which shows that the new system was firmly established when the Manuscript was written. The scribe occasionally *illuminates* the stops, enlarging them into decorative forms to harmonize with the general embellishments of the page. Plate III contains three striking examples of this curious innovation. In the 2nd, 4th and 7th lines from the foot of the page will be seen quaint ornaments of rectangular outline, intruding, as it were, immediately after the words *seniores, profetissa,* and *ihm.* They have probably been regarded, up till now, as mere instances of the stray decorative features which are scattered broadcast through the whole volume. Their position, however, in places where a full stop is actually required, and where there is no trace of any other punctuation marks to be seen, shows them to be nothing more or less than enlarged forms of the single dots which was one of the recognized methods of indicating the end of a sentence in early Celtic manuscript (see page 49). Plate X, at the end of line 4, furnishes another example; and plate XV contains yet another, though of much smaller proportions, following the word *mihi.* These strange instances of decorated punctuation would seem to me to have been introduced deliberately with a view to drawing special attention to the recently adopted rectangular punctuation signs; and it is hardly conceivable that liberties such as these would have been taken by any scribe unless the new system of pointing had been generally adopted at the time when he had the work in hand. If this be the case, it must follow that the date of the Manuscript should be ascribed to a period which cannot possibly be earlier than the latter end of the ninth century.

I have added a little to the Introduction bearing on the contest that continued for nearly a thousand years between the Byzantine and the Celtic modes of embellishment in the field of artistic illumination, and have touched, though lightly, on the superb results that sprang from the final union of the two contending forces. Also a few trivial oversights have been corrected in the letterpress of the original edition.

EDWARD SULLIVAN, 1920

THE BOOK OF KELLS

by SIR EDWARD SULLIVAN, Bart

Its weird and commanding beauty; its subdued and goldless colouring; the baffling intricacy of its fearless designs; the clean, unwavering sweep of rounded spiral; the creeping undulations of serpentine forms that writhe in artistic profusion throughout the mazes of its decorations; the strong and legible minuscule of its text; the quaintness of its striking portraiture; the unwearied reverence and patient labour that brought it into being; all of which combined go to make up the Book of Kells, have raised this ancient Irish volume to a position of abiding pre-eminence amongst the illuminated manuscripts of the world. Many attempts have been made to reproduce its unique illuminations; and, so far as form and outline are concerned, the reproductions have been as far as possible successful. But all such efforts have up till now failed to give a living representation of its marvellous pages—for without its colour harmonies no reproduction can be regarded as adequate from the point of view of art. The last important attempt at reproduction in colour was made about forty years ago; but the scientific knowledge of the time was unequal to the strain sought to be put upon it. In the years which have since elapsed, the science of light, photography, and colour reproduction has made rapid advances towards an accuracy which was unknown when the earlier attempts were published; and it is only by the aid of such advancement that the production of the present volume has become possible.

In this respect the work now published differs from all its predecessors; for, though still distant from absolute perfection, the reproductions here given will be found to be infinitely closer to the originals in the important matter of actual colour than any of the so-called facsimiles which up to the present have been included in any published work. For this reason the present volume should not be regarded as in any sense a rival of the uncoloured reproductions which have already appeared of the Book of Kells. Its office is rather to supplement in colour what has already been accomplished by ordinary photography and monochrome; to add a new value to previous efforts with the assistance of the most recent methods and processes of polychromatic photography and colour-printing. Looked at from this standpoint one may fairly claim for the work here produced that it fills with some measure of satisfaction a gap in the pictorial history of Celtic illumination, and affords as it were a nearer view of one of the most interesting and beautiful manuscripts which have yet come from the hands of man.

The town of Kells, in County Meath in Ireland, lies some twenty miles west of Drogheda and the Irish Channel. It was known in days as early as St Patrick's in the Latinized form of Cenondae, bearing at a somewhat later date the name of Cenannus and Kenlis. Kennansa was its old Irish appellation. Within its narrow precincts to-day there are still standing three very ancient and well-known Irish stone crosses with characteristic carvings on them; an old church, the rebuilt remains of which date from the year 1578; a round tower—one of the many to be found still in Ireland; and a building which has long been described as the House of St Columb.

Of the famous Monastery of Cenannus, or Kells, no trace remains—either of wall or foundation—but persistent tradition, with a strength that not infrequently outlasts both stone and mortar, has ascribed the founding of this vanished monastic institution to St Columba. Irish historians have fixed the date of its foundation as about A.D. 550.

Columba himself, otherwise known as Colum Cille, i.e. Columb of the Church, was born in the north-west of Ireland about A.D. 521. He is represented, according to ancient chronicle, as having resigned his hereditary claim on the kingship of the island with the object of devoting himself to a monastic life. About the year 553 he founded a monastery at Durrow, in central Ireland, which became, as the Venerable Bede has stated, his most important establishment in that country. He withdrew from his native land to Iona in A.D. 563, which island, afterwards known as Hy-Columkille, became, through the missionary exertions of himself and his successors of the abbatial see, the radiating centre of Christian civilization in the north of Britain, and the chosen burial place of the Kings of Pictland and Scotland. For this reason it is that Shakespeare, as we are reminded by Sir John Gilbert in his introduction to *National Manuscripts of Ireland*, tells us of King Duncan's body being

> carried to Colmekill,
> The sacred store-house of his predecessors,
> And guardian of their bones
> *Macbeth*, ii. 4.

19

An ancient Irish legend gives the reason why St Columba left his native land, and shows us, incidentally, a vivid picture of the militant churchman of those early days. During a sojourn with St Finnan, in Ulster, Columba borrowed his psalter, and copied it furtively in his church, with the aid of miraculous light in the night time. Finnan demanded the copy, but Columba refused to give it up, and the matter was submitted for judgment to Diarmaid, Monarch of Ireland, at Tara. Diarmaid, with the rough and ready justice of a new Solomon, decided that as to every cow belongs her calf, so to every book belongs its copy. A sanguinary battle was the result; but the copy remained with him who made it. It was known in later times as *Cathach*, from the Irish *cath*, a battle; and was preserved with much veneration by Columba's kindred. This psalter is now in the collection of the Royal Irish Academy, Dublin.

However, whether Columba or another was the actual founder of this early centre of Irish Christianity at Durrow, the place does not seem to have attained any great importance until the opening of the ninth century, when the marauders from northern Europe—Danes, Frisians, Norwegians, Swedes, Livonians, and such like—poured down upon the Irish ecclesiastical colony in Iona,

> and the godless hosts
> Of heathen swarming o'er the northern sea

drove the community of that island-sanctuary to seek a place of asylum farther west.

Some time between A.D. 802 and 815, when Cellach, the nineteenth successor of Columba, was Abbot of Iona, he fled for refuge to the monastery at Kells, and with his aid a new town of Colum Cille was erected there; and this, from that time forward, became the chief station of the Columban community—the Abbot of Kells being invariably acknowledged as the legitimate successor of St Columba. The names of both Columba and St Patrick are still legible on one of the ancient stone crosses to be seen at Kells. Colum Cille is commemorated as one of the three patron saints of Ireland on June the 9th, the anniversary of his death in the year 597.

Whether or not the famous Book of Kells, or, as it is often called, the Book of Colum Cille, was written and illuminated in the ancient town of Kells is a question still unsolved. The last few leaves of the Manuscript, which in all probability would have furnished us with full information as to scribe, illuminator, and place of origin, have been missing for many years.

The history of Kells and its Abbey from late in the ninth century to the end of the tenth is a tale of continuous struggle against foreign and domestic aggression.[1] In 899 the Abbey was sacked and pillaged. In 918 the Danes plundered Kells, and laid the church level with the ground. Rebuilt, it was again spoiled and pillaged by the Danes in 946. Three years later, Godfrey, son of Sitric, plundered the Abbey. In 967 the town and Abbey were pillaged by the King of Leinster's son, supported by the Danes; but the allied forces were assailed and defeated by Domnald O'Neill, King of Ireland. Only a year later the Abbey and town were despoiled by a united force of Danes and Leinster people; while in 996 the Danes of Dublin made yet another pillaging raid on both the town and Abbey. How the Gospels of St Columba survived this century of violence and spoliation it is impossible to say: we only know that they were preserved in the church at Kells in the year 1006, when, according to the earliest historical reference to the Manuscript itself, 'the large Gospel of Colum Cille' in its cover of gold studded with precious stones, 'the chief relic of the western world,' was stolen by night from the greater church at Kells, and found, after a lapse of some months, concealed under sods, destitute of its gold-covered binding.[2] It is not unlikely that most of the leaves now missing from the Manuscript disappeared at the same time.

Many of the palæographers who have made a study of the Kells Manuscript, agree in thinking that Giraldus Cambrensis has described this identical volume in a passage in his *Topographia Hiberniæ*. Writing in the twelfth century he gives an account of a wonderful manuscript which was shown to him at Kildare. He records that he had seen nothing more marvellous than the book in question, which, according to information given to him at the time, had been written from the dictation of an angel in the days of the Virgin (St Brigit). Giraldus undoubtedly has described an illuminated manuscript of great beauty which, so far as its general contents go, might have been the Book of Kells. He lavishes the highest praise on its brilliant colouring, on the endless variety of its figures, on the elaborate intricacies of its interlaced ornamentation—all of which, as he tells us, one would be ready to pronounce the work of angelic, and not human skill. Going into minuter detail, he continues: 'On one page you see the face of God, drawn in godlike fashion—in another, the forms of the Evangelists with either six, four, or two wings.'[3] When it is remembered that Giraldus spent many years, early and late in

1 Archdall's *Monasticon Hibernicum*.

2 Annals of Ulster, *sub anno* 1006.

3 *Hic maiestatis vultum videas divinitus impressum; hinc misticas evangelistarum formas, nunc senas, nunc quaternas, nunc binas alas habentes.*

life, as a student at the University of Paris, where it is probable he had become acquainted with a more modern type of illuminated miniatures, it seems difficult to believe that he could have been alluding in the last quoted passage to the more or less crude figure representations of the Saviour contained in the Book of Kells. Besides, there are no 'forms of the Evangelists' to be found in the Manuscript as it exists to-day that have either six or four wings;[1] nor, indeed, is there any convincing reason suggested why the Book of Kells should have been found at Kildare. It is perfectly obvious, too, from intrinsic evidence that the Kells Manuscript was produced at a period when Celtic illuminative art had reached its very highest development; and it is therefore plain that *it* was not produced in the lifetime of St Brigit (A.D. 453–523), whatever the volume may have been which Giraldus has described. Besides, it is hardly credible that Cambrensis, if referring to the Book of Kells, should have omitted all mention of the remarkable loss and recovery of the manuscript, the details of which had in his time been well known for at least two hundred years.

One can only conclude that the book which the historian did see was one of the many beautiful illuminated manuscripts that have since disappeared, though not the Kells volume; and that commentators have been somewhat too ready to adopt without much investigation a theory for which there seems to be but very little evidential support.

At the time of the dissolution of the monasteries the establishment at Kells was surrendered to the Crown by its last Abbot, Richard Plunket. The instrument under which this surrender was effected, dated 18th November 1539, is entered on the Rolls of the Chancery of Ireland, 31 Henry VIII. The famous manuscript of the Gospels itself, which seems to have survived in an almost miraculous fashion the unending incursions and pillage of many centuries, found its way shortly after the surrender of the monastery into the hands of one Gerald Plunket of Dublin, a kinsman possibly of the last Abbot. During the time the volume was in his possession he inscribed some notes which are still legible on its pages, showing that portions were lacking at the end of the book even in his day. On an early leaf he writes: 'This worke doth passe all men's conyng that now doth live in any place. I doubt not there . . . anything but that ye writer hath obtained God's grace. G.P.' Another of his notes, dated 27th August, 1568, purports to give the number

1 If the words *evangelistarum formas* can be made to refer to the Evangelistic Symbols (and not to the representations of the Evangelists), it is true that some of them have what seem to be four wings. In no case do they appear with six.

22

of the leaves then in the volume; but under these words Bishop Ussher has written: 'August 24 1621. I reckoned the leaves of this booke and found them to be in number 344. He who reckoned before me counted six score to the hundred. Ja Ussher, Midensis elect.'[1]

Ussher, who was commissioned by James I to collect antiquities relating to the British Church, acquired, amongst other rare possessions, the Book of Kells. It was included in the portion of his collection which was transferred to Trinity College, Dublin, five years after his death, in the year 1661; since which time it has been the chief treasure of the University Library. Housed as it then was, one might have expected that a volume of so notorious, not to say sacred, a character would have enjoyed inviolable sanctuary. Unhappily, what Norseman and Dane had failed to effect in early and wilder centuries was accomplished by an ignorant and mischievous bookbinder, some hundred years ago; and under the barbarous hands of this craftsman many of the outer margins of its priceless illuminations have been 'trimmed' out of existence, as may be seen by looking at the plates reproduced in this volume.

TRINITY COLLEGE, DUBLIN

The Manuscript in its present state consists of 339 leaves of thick, finely glazed vellum, measuring, in their now cropped condition, 13 by 9½ inches. The number of lines of text to a page of the Gospels is in general not more than 19 nor less than 17, the space occupied by the writing being 10 by 7 inches. On a few of the pages the writing is in a peculiar semi-cursive hand, but as a rule it is of the fine, clear character shown in plates III and X.

THE MANUSCRIPT

The first leaf—too rubbed to furnish a reproduction of a satisfactory kind—is surrounded by an ornamental border, and is divided vertically into two divisions, one containing a number of Hebrew words with their Latin equivalents, and the other occupied by the Evangelical Symbols. These symbols, which were adopted at an early period in the history of Christianity, are as follows: The Man, or Angel, stands for St Matthew, figurative of his emphasizing the human side of Christ; the Lion for St Mark, as he has set forth the power and royal dignity of Christ; the Calf, or sacrificial victim, for St Luke, as his Gospel illustrates the priesthood of the Saviour; and the Eagle for St John, the Evangelist who soars to heaven, as St Augustine puts it, and gazes on the light of immutable truth with keen and un-dazzled eyes. In the present instance these are all unhappily much worn by attrition,

1 *National Manuscripts of Ireland*, J. T. Gilbert's introduction. The words *Midensis elect* refer to Ussher's recent election to the Bishopric of Meath.

but enough is visible to show that books are held by each of the symbolical figures.

The next eight pages are filled with what are known as the Eusebian Canons. They take their name from Eusebius, Bishop of Cæsarea, a well-known Church historian. Before his time a Harmony of the Gospels had been constructed by Ammonius of Alexandria, about A.D. 220, in which St Matthew's Gospel was taken as the standard, and parallel passages from the other Gospels were set out side by side with it. Eusebius improved on his predecessor's plan; his object being to set forth the mutual relation of the four evangelical narratives, and not merely to furnish illustrations to certain passages from other sources, as in the marginal references in modern Bibles. The method of interpreting the lettering in these Canons, dependent as it is on certain sectional divisions of the Gospels specially devised by the author, is too intricate to go into here.

PLATE I   As will be seen in plate I, the Eusebian Canons are written in narrow columns, framed as it were by decorative pillars on which a considerable amount of characteristic ornament has been lavished. The open spaces above the pillars contain the Evangelical Symbols, agreeing in number with the number of the Evangelists in the several Canons. The decorative surroundings of these eight pages are different in each page. In two cases the ornamentation is of quite a simple nature, and little in keeping with the general character of this portion of the Manuscript.

The next few pages of the Manuscript would seem to have been left blank when the book was originally written. They now contain several charters in the Irish language, embodying grants of lands from King Melaghlin of Meath to the Abbey of Kells, the Bishop of Meath and the Church of Kells, dated between A.D. 1024 and the twelfth century. Their insertion on these pages was obviously intended to provide for their greater security. They have been printed by the Irish Archæological Society in the *Miscellany*, volume I, in the original Irish, with a translation and notes by Mr O'Donovan; and are believed to be the only extant specimens of legal deeds in the Irish language dating from before the Norman invasion.

PLATE II   Folio 7 verso, which follows, contains the full-page illustration of the Virgin and Child, on plate II, which Professor Westwood remarks[1]: 'This singular composition is interesting from the proof it affords of the veneration of the Virgin Mary in the early Irish Church; the large size in which she is represented, as well as the glory round her head (which singularly bears three small crosses), evidently indicating the high respect with which the Mother of Christ was regarded. The infant Saviour, it will be observed, is destitute of the nimbus; the chair or throne on which the

1 *Palæographia Sacra Pictoria*: Book of Kells.

24

Virgin is seated is not devoid of elegance, terminating above in the dog's head with an immensely elongated interlaced tongue.[1] The drawing of the whole is entirely puerile, whilst the ingenuity displayed in the intricate patterns of the sides and upper part of the drawing is quite remarkable. This singular interlacing of the limbs of human figures is peculiarly characteristic of the Irish MSS, and it is accordingly found in the Gospels of MacRegol and the Book of St Chad. The instrument held by the Angel at the right hand of the foot of the drawing is worthy of remark, being analogous to one of the sceptres held by St Luke in the Book of St Chad.'

The significance intended to be conveyed by the large size of the Virgin's figure finds a curious parallel in the sculptures still to be seen on the ancient monolith cross which stands close to St Columba's house at Kells. The rude figure of Christ there represented is much larger than the attendant figures. It was a form of denoting importance frequently employed in early Irish art. A singular feature of this picture of the Virgin is the group of six persons whose heads are shown in the small panel crossing the framework at the right-hand side. They are all turned away from the principal figure. Westwood, who finds it difficult to comprehend the object of their introduction, says that he knows no other instance of such an addition in the miniatures of the Virgin and Child. It will be noticed that by some curious error both the feet of the Virgin are right feet, while those of the Child are both left.

The pages which follow, extending to folio 25, contain the *breves causae*, i.e. chapter headings, and *argumenta*, i.e. summaries, appertaining to each of the four Gospels. Some of these pages are inscribed in a more recent hand and in variously coloured inks. This preliminary matter was a very frequent addition to Gospel MSS of and about the period of the Book of Kells. Coming as it did immediately before the Gospel itself, it was not unnaturally made the subject of much fine illumination. The first of these introductory pages breaks out amidst a magnificent wealth of intricate illumination in the words *Nativitas XPI in Bethlem Judeae Magi munera offerunt et infantes interficiuntur Regressio*: 'The birth of Christ in Bethlehem of Judea; the wise men present gifts; the slaying of the children; the return'. The more modern writing at the foot of the page, repeating these same words, is

[1] It is difficult to think that Westwood (and the late Dr Abbott, who took the same view) can here be right. The dog in the Bible had a notoriously evil reputation, being 'unclean' under the Old Law, and would hardly have been selected as an ornament for the Virgin's throne. The head can surely be no other than that of the Lion, which also appears at the end of two of the columns in plate I, and is found as a border terminal in plates VI and XI, not to mention other places throughout the manuscript. There may possibly be in plate II, an allusion to Solomon's throne (I Kings x, 19), where two lions had a place beside the stays of the seat.

believed to be in the hand of Gerald Plunket, possibly a relative of the last abbot of the monastery of Kells. It was from him that the volume passed into the possession of Archbishop Ussher, from whom, as already mentioned, it came to the library of Trinity College, Dublin.

PLATE III   Folio 19 verso, depicted in plate III, contains a portion of the 'Argument' to the Gospel of St John. This page, which contains some characteristic peculiarities common to early Irish manuscripts, reads as follows:

exponitur ut sciendi desiderio collocato Et
quaerentibus fructus laboris et deo magiste
rii doctrina servetur

ZACHA
riae sacerdotii appa
ruit angelus et adnuntiavit ei filium iohan
nem Et idem mariae adnuntiavit angelus
filium ihesum C *toribus Et acci*
Nativitatem ihesu adnuntiat angelus pas
pit simeon puerum ihesum Et benedixit
deum et de anna profetissa C *bat*
Annorum duodecim ihesus in templo doce
Seniores C *tismum poeniten*
Ubi iohannis baptizat populum bap

The symbol C, known in Irish MSS as 'head under the wing' or 'turn under the path'—which, as will be seen, occurs three times on this page—indicates that the words immediately following it are to be read after the end of the next full line. The first of the above passages in which it occurs will therefore read:

. . . *adnuntiavit angelus filium ihesum Nativitatem ihesu adnuntiat angelus pastoribus Et accipit simeon,* etc.

The 'turn under the path' occasionally takes other shapes. A curious instance of its altered form is to be found in the Pater Noster, folio 297 verso, where it appears at the beginning of the half-line in the figure of a small man apparently in the act of jumping, with one of his legs cocked up and the other turned down towards the following line of the text.

From folios 20 recto to 26 verso the text is much varied by the use of black, scarlet and mauve inks. In folio 23, front and back, the writing is all in mauve,

26

excepting the last line of the verso and the ornamental initials, while touches of red and yellow are introduced for decoration. This portion, in fact, presents us with a handwriting totally different from that which precedes and follows it. It looks as if the original had possibly been lost and was replaced by the work of a later and much inferior artist. The initials in these twelve pages are not distinguished by any special excellence.

Following the twentieth leaf (misplaced as some maintain) are two grants of land, in Irish, for a consideration of three ounces of gold. After these come the Evangelical Symbols again, as reproduced in plate IV, folio 27 verso. The central PLATE IV and some of the other panels in the borders of this page contain miniature work of an astounding perfection.

St Matthew's portrait with its surrounding border fills the back of the next leaf, plate V. As will be seen in the illustration, the Lion symbol of St Mark shows its PLATE V head at each side of the back of the throne; while the heads of the Calf and Eagle of St Luke and St John appear behind the extremities of the seat. The spreading ornaments filling the spandrels of the arch are modelled on the flabellum, an instrument used from an early period in the Eastern Church for the purpose of keeping flies from the altar.

The opening words of St Matthew's Gospel, *Liber generationis*, one of the most notable instances of illumination in the Manuscript, fill the recto of folio 29, plate VI. The spiral ornamentation and the general colour harmony of this very beautiful PLATE VI page are particularly striking. Note, too, the curious and rarely relied on effect produced by the alteration of the colours in which the ground and the letters of the word *generationis* are depicted. The rudely-drawn figure standing in the lower left-hand corner is said to represent the Evangelist. The smaller and much more naturally drawn figure at the top may also be intended for him. The difference of execution in the two cases would, I suggest, almost justify the conclusion that the larger figure was a later addition in order to fill a space left vacant when the original artist had touched the Manuscript for the last time. I think, too, that we can almost see from the illumination itself the very place where he was hurried from his work. There are many unfinished portions in the whole page; for instance, the small face to the left of the upper limb of the L, the piece of the border of the same limb just above and to the right of the face, and possibly the space into which the right elbow of the upper figure projects. But more noticeable than all these is the unfinished condition of the intertwined letters ER in the circle which forms the lower portion of the antique and curiously formed B. The dark line surrounding the red

E is only half completed. The interruption of so very simple a feature of the work seems to tell a tale of perhaps even tragic significance.

PLATE VII   The Genealogy of Christ follows, extending to five pages. This portion of the Manuscript—like the illuminated page just referred to and some other pages to be mentioned later—has never been finished. It is nevertheless of extreme interest and great artistic value, as it shows us the very process adopted by the illuminator when at work. Folio 29 verso, for instance, gives us the mere text in two columns with seven finely traced plain circles added by way of incipient ornamentation. In folio 30 recto we find the same circles filled up in yellow as a ground, one only of them having a slight pattern added in red, while traces of lines are to be seen round parts of the page. The back of this leaf shows the decoration in a further state of advance, corner ornaments of winged bird-like creatures being lightly sketched in pale mauve and yellow, while some of the central circles are ornamented. A still further advance is disclosed on the page which follows (folio 31 recto), dots in red being added round a central lozenge, a couple of small illuminated initials being also introduced. There are other instances here and there through the Kells Manuscript of pages being left in an incomplete condition. Obvious examples are to be found in the upper portion of the large L in plate VI, as already mentioned, and again in plate VII, where the blank spandrels to right and left of the head of the central figure strike a note of strong discord amidst the colour harmony of their rich surroundings. Again, in the case of the Eusebian Canons, at folio 4 verso, the spandrels of the upper arch have been rudely filled in by some later and very inferior artist; pale blue triangles, roughly decorated with red, being introduced on a mauve-purple ground, the whole clashing unpleasantly with the extremely fine ornamentation of the remainder of the page.

It is, of course, now impossible to guess with anything approaching certainty how some of the illuminations came to be left unfinished—the death of a great artist before his work was done; the turmoils and uncertainty of the age; the necessity for keeping so precious a treasure in concealment when piracy and plunder were always to be feared, will suggest themselves as possibly accounting for these strange lacunæ—but none of these explanations is completely satisfactory. I shall refer to the subject again when dealing with the much disputed question of the actual date of the manuscript.

'DOUBTFUL   The so-called 'Doubtful Portrait' on folio 32 verso, plate VII, following the
PORTRAIT'   Genealogy is, according to Westwood,[1] 'evidently misplaced, and is intended for

1 *Palæographia Sacra Pictoria: op. cit.*

28

one of the two Evangelists whose portraits are wanting', that is, St Mark or St Luke. The principal figure, as may be seen in the illustration, sits on a chair or throne, and holds a book in the left hand, which is covered by the robe. Westwood here rightly draws attention to the curly flaxen hair, the short stiff beard, the misplaced ears, and the right hand, which appears to be in the act of benediction, with the first and second fingers extended in the Roman manner, the feet evidently wearing sandals, the two peacocks standing on plants in vases, and some other features, which certainly render the picture one of exceptional interest. Gerald Plunket, when the volume was in his possession, had written the words *Jesus Christus* in the blank spandrels to the right and left of the head of the figure. The writing has since been removed, leaving the white spaces somewhat staringly vacant, but no doubt in the very condition they were in when the illumination was interrupted. The presence of the cross above, as the Rev Mr Stanford Robinson remarks,[1] together with the colour of the vestments, the chalice-like cups, the vine, the peacock, and the four angelic beings, most of which are introduced into the decoration of the page, give grounds for Gerald Plunket's ascription. Petrie, too, took the portrait to be that of Christ, and for some reason described the page as 'the frontispiece of the Book of Kells'. Westwood opposed this view, pointing out, amongst other arguments, that the peacock was occasionally used in early gospels without any suggestion of symbolism. Dr Abbott, in his *Celtic Ornaments from the Book of Kells*, calls it 'Portrait of an Evangelist (St Mark or St Luke)', but without suggesting any reasons for his description. The title of Doubtful Portrait which has clung to the picture so long has in reality no justification whatever; and some additional and valid reasons, which seem to have been overlooked till now, may be suggested to show that the central figure is intended for either St Mark or St Luke, but certainly not for Christ.

The figure on folio 32 verso, plate VII, is obviously one of a series of four PLATE VII portraits of the Evangelists, which, judging by the surviving three, are all clearly stamped with a similarity of artistic treatment. In each case the Evangelist holds a book in his hand, and occupies a chair or throne in a sitting position. In both plates v and VII the framework surrounding the portrait is identical in the matter of outline of design and general composition. St John's picture, plate XVIII, though its frame differs somewhat from the other two, is, by reason of certain features which are common to all three, sufficiently allied to the others to justify its inclusion in the series. The fact, too, that the head of the latter portrait is surrounded by so

1 *Celtic Illuminated Art*, Dublin, 1908.

magnificent a nimbus, while that of plate VII is distinguished by only a very small cross, would seem to preclude the possibility of the latter being intended as a portrait of the Saviour. The presence of the two peacocks, the chalices (if they be such, which is very questionable) and the vine, does not seem to add any great force to the view which Mr Robinson favours, all three being iconographic symbols which are entirely appropriate to the decoration of any portrait of a writer of one of the Gospels. I may also mention that 'the four angelic beings' partly relied on by Mr Robinson consist of two winged figures, and two that are obviously of a human type, and have no wings at all. There is the manifest fact, too, that this page was left in an unfinished state. The spandrels to right and left of the head of the main figure are absolutely blank, and it is to my mind impossible

PLATE VII to believe that they were intended to remain so. The borders enclosing the spandrels are also unfinished, as will be seen on comparing them with the same borders lower down. Other evidences of incompleteness will appear on a close study of the exterior corner-pieces of the astoundingly beautiful border. It will be noticed that the interior details of the one at the left top are carried out in every way worthily of the master-hand that did the greater portion of the very intricate patterns with which the page is filled. Look now at the remaining three corner-pieces, and consider the comparatively clumsy and unrefined way in which they are filled in. Although the three are themselves more or less of the same design and colour tone, they are all utterly out of harmony with the first, and form a distinct blot on this most beautifully illuminated page. Look, then, at the four corner-pieces of the consort portrait, plate V, and see how harmoniously they are executed, both in colour and design, and it will be at once understood that the three inconsistent and badly executed corners of plate VII must have been left by the greater artist as blank as the spandrel spaces themselves. Further than this, I am strongly inclined to think that the discs which touch the feet of the main figure have also been filled in by the later and inferior artist. A comparison with the similarly situated discs in plate V, which contain some very fine work, will go far, I think, to justify such a conclusion. The outer trivialities in the way of decoration which are to be seen beyond the corner-pieces in plate VII, are only too obviously the work of an inferior hand. Is it, then, in all the circumstances conceivable that, if this were a portrait of Christ, it would ever have been left unfinished? Can we imagine that in its manifestly patched condition it would have been used, as Petrie thought it was, as 'the frontispiece of the Book of Kells'?

PLATE VIII Plate VIII shows the eight-circled cross, a superb example of the most intricate

30

and delicate ornamentation. It is the only specimen of this type of design in the Kells Manuscript, but it has its counterpart in the Book of Lindisfarne,[1] the Celtic illuminations of which can alone of all Irish or Anglo-Irish MSS be compared for beauty, design or execution, with the pages of the Book of Kells. Westwood thinks that each of the Kells Gospels was preceded by a similarly ornamented leaf, which has disappeared.

PLATE IX

Facing this eight-circled cross is what is known as the Monogram page, plate IX, containing the three opening words of St Matthew i. 18, *XPI [Christi] autem generatio*— the whole forming, as Professor Westwood rightly remarks, the most elaborate specimen of calligraphy which was perhaps ever executed. The late Rev Dr Todd has suggested, with some considerable likelihood, that the ornamental line which runs above the predominant letter is intended to present the usual mark of contraction, placed over the shortened word *XPI [Christi]*. 'It may be observed,' he adds, 'that the page before us contains almost all the varieties of design to be found in Celtic art. These are usually spoken of as twofold: first, arbitrary or geometrical—of which there occur on the page before us the divergent pattern known as the trumpet-pattern, the triquetra, the interlaced curved bands, the knot, and the designs formed of eight lines; secondly, patterns derived from natural forms—foliage, birds, reptiles, fish, quadrupeds, imaginary or monstrous animals, and man.'[2] Noticeable amidst such an extraordinary profusion of decorative forms are the three angels to the left, two of whom hold books in one hand and blossom sceptres in the other, the remaining one grasping two of these sceptres—which, in the latter instance, spread into a trefoil pattern. A strange group of animals will be observed between the bottom of the P and the up line of the X—two rats nibbling the Eucharistic bread under the eyes of a pair of cats. The Rev Mr Robinson suggests that there may be in this design an allusion to unworthy receivers, and the impending judgment which awaited such profanation. Slightly to the right will be seen an otter-like creature with a fish in its mouth. The animal has been described by some critics as rat-like, but its size, shape, and colouring are all against the suggestion. The four diamond panels in the upper portion of the P, which are apparently left plain, are in reality each made up of sixteen small diamond sections most delicately ornamented with key patterns.

The observations of Johan A. Brunn[3] on this page excellently supplement such

1 In the Cottonian Library, British Museum.
2 *Vetusta Monumenta*, Society of Antiquaries, London, 1869.
3 *An Enquiry into the Art of the Illuminated MSS. of the Middle Ages*, Stockholm, 1897.

quotations as are given above in reference to it:

'There is a beautiful instance in the Book of Kells, presumably surpassing, as a piece of decoration, anything to be met with in any other written book. It is a page to discourage even the most accomplished and most enthusiastic of modern draughtsmen. In nine cases out of ten he will break down before his work is half finished; or, if he should really succeed in completing it, he will have to expend upon it an amount of time and labour out of all proportion to the apparent result of his work. Mr Digby Wyatt made an attempt, and had to give it up. Professor J. O. Westwood, who was a great admirer of Irish art and at the same time a skilled draughtsman, went to work with no better result. And he was assuredly not one to be discouraged by difficulties arising from variety of colours and intricacy of design. No one who has had an opportunity of examining the leaves of the big volume containing the Professor's original tracings and now deposited in the Ashmolean Museum at Oxford can have failed to be struck by the minute accuracy of his delineations and the immense pains taken in rendering even the most complicated passages of Celtic ornament. And yet the copying of the monogram page of the Book of Kells was, if not beyond his powers, at least too long and serious an affair to be duly brought to completion. We are indebted to Miss Margaret Stokes, the accomplished writer on Celtic antiques, for possessing at last, a copy[1] perfectly finished and worthy of an original which the same author, in a brilliant passage[2] referring to its unique variety of design, has signalized as "an epitome of Irish art." '

The text of the Gospel according to St Matthew follows in large uncial and minuscule combined, initial letters of a highly ornamental character being freely used all through, but without any repetition of design. Other instances of elaborate decoration on a larger scale are furnished later on by a drawing of Christ seized by two Jews (Matthew xxvi. 50) on folio 114 recto, and on the verso of the same leaf the full-page illumination embodying the words *Tunc dicit illis ihs omnes vos scan [dalum* etc]. These words have been written in again in a later hand (now a good deal rubbed), as if they had been found difficult to read in their illuminated form.

PLATE X   Plate x, folio 104 recto, furnishes an excellent example of the general run of the

1 Now deposited in the National Museum of Ireland, Dublin. A chromo-lithographic reproduction, which, however, is somewhat defective in softness and harmony of colour, may be seen in *Vetusta Monumenta.*

2 Margaret Stokes, *Early Christian Art in Ireland*, London, 1887, page 13.

32

written text, with such small illuminated initials and added decorative curiosities as occur so frequently throughout the whole Manuscript. The page is also useful for showing in a brief way the kind of variations from the Vulgate that are to be found everywhere in the Book of Kells. The extract is from Matthew xxiv. 19–24. The two versions are set side by side for the purpose of convenient comparison:

BOOK OF KELLS	VULGATE
Vae autem praegnantibus Et nutriantibus in illis diebus.	*Vae autem praegnantibus, et nutrientibus in illis diebus.*
Orate autem ut non fiat fuga vestra hime vel sabbato.	*Orate autem ut non fiat fuga vestra in hieme, vel sabbato.*
Erit enim tunc tribulatio magna qualis non fuit ab initio mundi usque modo neque fiet.	*Erit enim tunc tribulatio magnaqualis non fuit ab initio mundi usque modo, neque fiet.*
Et nisi braeviati* fuissent dies illi non fieret salva om- nis caro sed propter electos brae- viabuntur* dies illi.	*Et nisi breviati fuissent dies illi, non fieret salva omnis caro: sed propter electos breviabuntur dies illi.*
Tunc si quis vobis dixerit ecce hic Christus aut illic nolite credere	*Tunc si quis vobis dixerit: Ecce hic est Christus, aut illic: nolite credere.*
Surgent enim saeudo* Christi Et saeudo profetae et dabunt signa magna et prodigia ita in errorem movantur si fieri potest etiam	*Surgent enum pseudochristi, et pseu- doprophetae: et dabunt signa magna, et prodigia, ita ut in errorem inducantur (si fieri potest) etiam electi.*

Plate xi, folio 124 recto, exhibits the commencement of verse 38 of the 27th chapter of St Matthew, *Tunc crucifixerant XPI cum eo duos latrones* (Then were there two thieves crucified with him). The XPI which seems to belong to the sentence, is, as pointed out by Sir John Gilbert, probably only the medieval note- mark composed of the monogram of *Christi*, which was arbitrarily used to call attention to remarkable passages. It was known as the Chrismon. The Vulgate reading of this passage takes a more accurate Latin form in *Tunc crucifixi sunt*, this being one of the many differences in reading between that edition and the version   PLATE XI

* The curious arrow-head symbol under the starred words which, as will be seen in plate x, occurs three times on this page, represents the letter a. It is referred to again in the section dealing with the date of the MS.

contained in the Book of Kells. Reference will be made later on to some more important variations existing between the two texts.

The Evangelical Symbols again occupy a prominent place at the opening of St
PLATE XII Mark's Gospel, folio 129 verso, plate XII, their decorative treatment differing completely from the corresponding page in the previous Gospel. Each of the figures here is furnished with a kind of sceptre. The whole is a most admirably balanced piece of artistic work, both in its decoration and drawing. The misplaced outside central ornament at the bottom is difficult to account for. It possibly represents an attempt to correct by balance the unequal length of the lower limbs of the inverted T panel in the border immediately above. I do not know of any other instance of an error of this kind in the Manuscript.

THE
'INITIUM
EVANGELII'
PAGE
PLATE XIII The first words of this Gospel, *Initium evangelii Ihu Xpi*, folio 130 recto, plate XIII, fill a whole page, the bold magnificence of the three letters INI being especially remarkable. The entire design is filled with the most characteristic details of Celtic ornament, but arranged with extraordinary originality. A studied comparison between it and the *Christi autem generatio*, or monogram page, plate IX, will show the astounding artistry of both, and at the same time exemplify the wide differences which lie between them. The Rev Mr Robinson points out the features of the *Initium* design which specially call for notice, and draws attention to 'the beautiful effect produced by the interlaced snakes at the four corners of the letter N. The three circles above the letters EVAN are filled with the heads of birds: the other circles above and below are filled with a curious heart-shaped design formed of spirals. The grotesque human figure at the top is held in the grasp of a dragon: under the cross of the T are the wings of two dragons.'

With his last sentence I cannot, however, agree, as I fail to see anything grotesque in the figure referred to. It is obviously a holy figure, as shown by the small circles and dots set in triangular groups with which the lower garments are decorated. I shall have some observations later on this very characteristic feature of robe-decoration in the Book of Kells. For the present I suggest strongly that the figure, so far from being grotesque, is intended for the Evangelist St Mark himself, in just the same way as the other small figures similarly introduced in plates VI and XIX are intended for the respective authors of the illuminated words with which they are surrounded. As to the 'dragon,' in the grasp of which the figure in plate XIII is stated to be held, I do not think it is a dragon. I believe it to be an animal much more appropriate to the surroundings, the symbolical lion of St Mark himself. A close examination of the plate will show that the saint is assisting the

34

lion in its efforts to devour the red serpent.[1] The very same contest, omitting the human figure, is depicted in the large illuminated T of the word *Tunc* in plate XI. The lion's head is the same in both cases, and so are the claws. The claws also correspond exactly with those on the lion in the Evangelical Symbols in plates IV and XII. The very unusual form of the g in *evangelii* should be noticed.

Another full-page illumination (though not amongst those illustrated here) of a strikingly different character of design comes later in the same Gospel, where a tessellated pattern is used with very telling effect. It contains the words of the 25th verse of chapter xv: *Erat autem hora ter* [*tia*]. The large blank spaces in this page strongly suggest that it was left in an unfinished state. The last page of this Gospel is decorated with two most singular dragon-like monsters, forming lateral diagonal ornaments to the page, an angel and a lion occupying the open side spaces.

St Luke's Gospel opens with a very striking example of illumination in which the PLATE XIV word *Quoniam* fills the whole of folio 188 recto, plate XIV. Some critics, and amongst them Professor Westwood, have suggested that the word is given here in a contracted form, viz. *Qniam*; but the u and o are both to be seen in the central diamond, the former as a v, and the o as a Greek ω, though somewhat angular in form. The crowd of figures intermixed with letters NIAM may possibly have been suggested by the words which follow—*multi conati sunt ordinare narrationem* (forasmuch as many have taken in hand, etc). The trumpet and spiral patterns are here exceptionally fine. The page has been badly mutilated by the former binder both at top and left-hand side. The verso of the leaf contains the words *Fuit in diebus Herodis*, which in their simplicity of decoration form a curious contrast to the first word of the Gospel.

Five pages are then occupied with the Genealogy of Christ, each line beginning PLATES with *Qui fuit* as illustrated in plates XV, XVI and XVII. The initials are all through XV–XVII interlaced with birds, dragons, beasts and snakes. At the bottom of one of these pages, plate XV, is, as Westwood observes,[2] 'an Irish warrior of the sixth century, having in his hand a little round shield (not a long pointed shield like that which the Norman warriors carried, reaching down to their feet) holding a long (?) spear with a spike at the bottom. . . . His breeches are prettily ornamented with three spirals, and that is the ordinary way in which the Celtic artists ornamented everything. I know of no other Gospel book which has such a series of letters at

1 If a lens is used for the purpose of examining the plates in the present volume it will be found that one of *moderate* capacity is more effectual than a strong magnifier.

2 'The Book of Kells', an Oxford lecture, 1886.

the commencement of each portion of the Genealogy, and this is carried on . . . with all that long series of names.'

PLATES
XV–XVII Folio 201 verso, introduces a distinctly humorous note amidst the stained-glass window solemnity attaching to the figure painting of the Manuscript—the same note that is supplied by gargoyles in the architecture of some centuries later. This page of the Genealogy, which in a general way resembles the pages reproduced in plates XV, XVI and XVII, contains a string of Q's with which are intertwined a number of droll and impish figures in various grotesque positions, with legs tucked under their arms, and tongues protruding. They pull each other's hair from behind, and one has his toe thrust under the nose of another figure in front. The uppermost of them even carries something resembling the air-bladder of pantomine; yet all the contortions of their limbs are contrived to fall in with the interlacings of the prevailing scheme of the design, a *tour de force*, as it were, of a big and genuinely human artist in holiday mood after months, or even years, of serious and reverent toil.

A singularly beautiful arabesque, the only example of its kind in the manuscript, fills the middle portion of the fifth of these pages from side to side, forming a terminal to the Genealogy. It is divided into two horizontal panels, the compartment to the right suggesting a vase and vine motif, that to the left containing two eagle-headed serpentine creatures whose wings are strangely woven into the general decoration. The whole is surmounted at the centre by the head and shoulders of a human figure wearing a moustache and triple pointed beard, his feet showing below. The entire composition forms one of the most striking instances of lacertine convolution and colour to be found in the volume.

The controversy of Christ and the Devil (not reproduced) fills folio 202 verso. The drawing here is apparently of a strangely barbarous character; but the draughtsman for all that seems to have been well aware of what was expected of him. The small size of the Devil is obviously intended to convey a suggestion of his powerlessness in the presence of the Saviour. It is noticeable, too, that Satan here has wings but no tail. The figures on the right of Christ are disciples; those above his head, angels. The execution of this page shows also very clearly that more than one artist was engaged on the illumination of the Book of Kells. The better of the two was an incomparable master of his art; the other possessed only very ordinary powers.

The whole page, *Jesus autem plenus S.S*, which faces the one just mentioned is also of inferior workmanship and design.

36

Speaking of the Gospels generally, Professor Westwood[1] has drawn attention to an un-Irish usage at the end of the Gospels in the Book of Kells. They do not here conclude with the word *finit*, the words at the end of St Luke being *Explicit evangelium secundum lucam incipit evangelium secundum johannem.*[2]

Folio 290 recto, is occupied by seven widely-spread lines of orange-red minuscule, with some rough attempts at illumination by the introduction of dashes of yellow, mauve, and purple. *Explicit evangelium secundum lucam* is twice repeated, followed by *Incipit evangelium secundum johannem.*

Folio 290 verso shows the Evangelical Symbols again, but in an altered form, at the beginning of St John's Gospel, the rectilinear frame border being worked into a profusion of decorative interlacements. The following leaf bears the portrait of St John (plate XVIII) with its glorious nimbus. The curious arrangement of the PLATE XVIII hair is particularly to be noticed, illustrating, as Petrie and others mention, the ancient habit of the Irish. The feet of the figure are enclosed in sandals. More especially deserving of attention are the writing materials with which the Evangelist is furnished. He holds in his hand a long pen, which is shown to be a quill by the feather ending, and at his right foot is a conical ink-pot. I shall have some further observations at a later stage on the writing and writing-materials made use of by the scribes who produced the manuscript. The so-called 'nail' in the right hand of the partially-concealed figure in plate XVIII is, I believe, a late addition, and resembles a lighted taper more than anything else. It will be observed that it is held in the hand and not driven through it as a nail would have been.

The opening words of St John's Gospel, *In principio erat Verbum et Verbum* fill the recto of folio 292. Plate XIX shows the splendidly decorative design into which PLATE XIX they are thrown. The four-circle groups forming the terminal ornaments of the IN are instances of the unlimited originality of the artist's decorative skill; while the extraordinary grace and intricacy of the setting of the letters RINCI are beyond all praise. It is possible that the combination of the C and I is intended to suggest a harper playing a harp: perhaps the fingers of the player, which seem to suggest the harp-strings, may have originated the idea. The figure at the top holding a book is, as in St Matthew's case, plate VI, plainly intended for the author of the Gospel which begins on this page—St John. The smaller figure, to the right, appears to be raising a conically-shaped cup to his lips.

The latter portion of this Gospel is wanting. The two closing lines on the recto of

1 *Palæographia Sacra Pictoria.*
2 Westwood has a misprint here reading *explicit* for *incipit.*

the last page (folio 339) are St John xvii. 5–6: *aput te Manifestum nomen tuum hominibus quos dedisti mihi de mundo. Tui*. Almost the whole of the text on the reverse side of the leaf has been rendered illegible by attrition—the last surviving words being *Pater sancte* which occur in the eleventh verse of chapter xvii.

No sufficient attention, so far as I am aware, has been drawn to the enormous hiatus in the original manuscript of which this sudden ending gives a striking proof. No less than four chapters and a half, containing some 152 verses, are missing from the end of St John, and 52 more from chapters xii and xiii. A dozen verses are also lacking in St Luke xii. Having regard to the average number of lines and words contained in each page of the Book of Kells, we find by a simple calculation that at least twenty-four leaves of text alone have disappeared from the book. It is possible, too, that there may have been some full-page illuminations included in the missing portion, so that, allowing an extra leaf for the colophon, and adding a few leaves which are obviously lost at the beginning of the book, together with the missing portrait of one of the Evangelists, we have a total loss of about twenty-nine folios, or fifty-eight pages. All but five of these must have been removed long before the manuscript came into the hands of Ussher. It is, indeed, more than likely that they had been lost five or six centuries before his time.

The one amongst these many wanted leaves, the loss of which is chiefly to be deplored, is that containing the colophon. It would probably have told when the work was regarded as finished, and might have furnished us with the name of the artist who conceived and wrought the unrivalled wonders of its illuminations.

The royal autographs of Queen Victoria (1849), Prince Albert (1849), and Prince Alfred (1861) are inscribed on one of the supplemental blank leaves at the beginning of the manuscript.

THE TEXT
OF THE
MANUSCRIPT
Interesting as are the decorative features of the Kells manuscript, the various readings of the actual text of the Gospels which it contains are of no less interest to students of Biblical history. It should be remembered that Christianity was introduced into Ireland at a very early date; though it is even now by no means certain whether it reached the country direct from the disciples of Irenæus at Lyons, or from the Roman or English missionaries during an early part of the period in which Great Britain had become a province of Rome. Owing probably to her remoteness from the rest of the civilized world, Ireland retained the primitive religious doctrines and discipline of the Church in their original forms for a much longer time than any other of the west-European communities. Amongst the

38

changes which the Irish Church was slow to recognize was the adoption in the sixth century of St Jerome's Latin translation of the Bible, commonly called the Vulgate, as the version authorized by the Church of Rome.[1] The more ancient Latin version, then displaced, is termed the Old Italic or Ante-Hieronymian; and to this version, with occasional modifications, the Irish Church continued to adhere until the beginning of the ninth century. The result was a mixed text, which was used in Ireland for a very considerable time after the adoption of the Vulgate by the authorities at Rome, a very remarkable instance of which mixed version is furnished by the Book of Kells itself—the text of which belongs to the Irish recension of St Jerome's version.

I have already (page 33 *ante*) illustrated the general nature of the variations between the Kells version and the Vulgate in an extract from St Matthew xxiv. They are in the main of a trivial kind and involve no questions of doctrine. In one very important instance, however, there is a much more serious conflict between the two versions, as the following passage from Westwood[2] will show:

'In the first place I may mention that I detected in it [the Book of Kells] the celebrated passage asserting the divinity of the Holy Ghost, which has hitherto been considered as unique in the Silver Gospels at Vercelli. It occurs in St John iii. 5, 6 (folio 297 verso), and is as follows: *Quod natum est ex carne caro est quia de carne natum est et quod natūm est ex spū (spiritu) sps̄ (spiritus) est quia ds̄ (divinus) sps̄ est et ex dō (domino) natus est.* These words were struck out by the Arians, and Father Simon asserted that there was no Latin manuscript in existence in which they were to be found.'

There are a considerable number of errors in orthography in the pages of the Irish manuscript, many of which have never been corrected. One important instance of correction is to be found on folio 219 recto, where the text of the preceding page, folio 218 verso has been erroneously repeated. Attention is drawn to the error by four obeli in red, running down the middle of the page between the lines, and others round the margins, and red lines about the corners. Peculiar spellings of words occur also. Amongst the more notable are *zabulus* and *diabulus*; *scandalis* for *sandaliis*; *thensaurus* for *thesaurus*; *Gychenna, hipochritae* and *chipochritae*; *cartam* for *quartam* and *beire* for *potum*.

1 The Golden Gospels, written on purple vellum for Ceolfrid, Abbot of Wearmouth, *c.* 700, were, as Quaritch states, the first Vulgate text seen in England (*Book Illumination during the Middle Ages*, 1889).

2 *Palæographia Sacra Pictoria: op. cit.*

The appended table of a few selected variants will show in a very general way how frequently and to what extent the readings of the two versions differ from one another. It will be noticed that whole passages are occasionally included in the Kells manuscript which are not found in the Vulgate:

Vulgate	Book of Kells
Caenantibus autem eis acceptit Iesus panem et benedixit ac fregit deditque discipulis suis et ait Accipite et comedite; hoc est Corpus meum.	*. . . . . accipit . . . . discipulis suis dicens accipite edite ex hoc omnes hoc est enim Corpus meum quod confringitur pro saeculi vita.*
Matthew xxvi. 26.	
Heli heli lema sabacthani.	*Heli heli laba sabacthani.*
Ib. xxvii. 46.	
Ceteri vero dicebant sine videamus an veniat Helias liberans eum.	*. . . Helias et liberaret eum. Alius autem accepta lancia pupungit latus ejus et exiit aqua et sangis [sic].*
Ib. xxvii. 49.	
Factum est autem in diebus illis exiit edictum a Caesare Augusto ut describeretur universus orbis.	*in illis diebus . . . accessare agusto ut censum profiterentur universi per orbem terrae.*
Luke ii. 1.	
ut profiteretur cum Maria desponsata sibi uxore praegnante.	*. . . sibi disponsata . . praegnante de spiritu sancto.*
Ib. ii. 5.	
et videbit omnis caro salutare dei.	*et videbitur maies [sic] domini.*
Ib. iii. 6.	
genimina viperarum.	*o generatio viperarum.*
Ib. iii. 7.	
adveniat regnum tuum: panem nostrum cotidianum da nobis cotidie.	*adveniat regnum tuum: fiat voluntas tua sicut in coelo et in terra, da nobis hodie.*
Ib. xi. 3.	

VULGATE	BOOK OF KELLS
(No corresponding passage.)	(At end of verse:)
Ib. iii. 25.	*Susciperunt ergo Iesum et portans crucem ducebatur.*
et depositum involvit sindone, et posuit eum in monumento exciso, in quo nondum quisquam positus fuerat.	*. . . in sindone munda . . . . . . et imposito eo imposuit monumento lapidem magnam.*
Ib. xxiii. 53.	
Et cum dixisset, statim discessit ab eo lepra, et mundatus est.	[After *mundatus est*] *et inspiciens Iesus austri vultu eicit eum.*
Mark i. 17.	
grex porcorum magnus pascens.	*. . . . . . pascensium* [*sic*].
Ib. v. 11.	
et videt tumultum.	*vidit cumuultum* [*sic*].
Ib. v. 38.	
Et angariaverunt praetereuntem quempiam.	*. . . . angarizaverunt . . . . .*
Ib. xv. 21.	
Quod natum est ex carne caro est, et quod natum est ex spiritu spiritus est.	*Quod natum est ex carne caro est quia de carne natum est, et quod natum est ex spiritu spiritus est quia deus spiritus est et ex deo natus est.*[1]
John iii. 6.	

Of all questions in any way connected with the Book of Kells for which critics have sought a solution, there is none of greater interest than the question of its date. Going, as it does, deep into the mysteries in which the origin and execution of early Irish manuscript illumination have for many centuries been veiled, it has naturally stimulated students of medieval decorative art to propound at least some theory which would fix within a century or two the period in which so perfect an example of miniature ornament can have been produced. Indications to suggest its time of

THE DATE OF THE MANUSCRIPT

---

1 As will be seen, page 39 *ante*, Westwood misreads the contractions *ds* and *dō* as *divinus* and *domino* instead of *deus* and *deo*.

birth have been sought in all possible directions. Historical evidence is of little assistance. The Manuscript itself fails us where, conceivably, it might have helped us most, for the page that should have told its story is unfortunately no longer there. The style of its writing, the particular version of the Scriptures it contains, the nature of its decorative embellishments, its orthography, pigments, ink, and even the manner in which its vellum was prepared, have one and all engaged the close attention of those who know much on all these matters; yet in spite of all that has been written on the subject, no one can say with any certainty to-day whether it belongs to the sixth or the ninth century. The early commentators on the Manuscript ascribe it without hesitation to the sixth century, O'Donovan and Dr Todd being amongst them. Miss Stokes and Professor Middleton say it belongs to the latter half of the seventh century, and in agreement with them are Westwood and Sir E. M. Thompson. The Rev Mr Stanford Robinson, relying largely on a comparison of its text and ornamentation with those of the Book of Durrow, thinks it cannot be placed earlier than the eighth century; while Dr T. K. Abbott assigns it to that century also. Dr E. H. Zimmermann, in the prospectus of a comprehensive work which was in preparation in 1914, *Die Vorkarolingischen Miniaturen*, dates the Kells Manuscript *circa* A.D. 700, making it more or less contemporary with the Book of Durrow. A study of the initials of the latter manuscript satisfies him that *its* date is about a century later than usually believed. Sir John Gilbert gives it any time between A.D. 600 and 900; while Brunn holds that it was produced in the ninth century under the influence of the early renaissance in the reign of Charlemagne. The latest view expressed on the subject is that of Mr R. A. S. Macalister,[1] who seeks to show that the Book of Lindisfarne—which he suggests, and most people believe, was earlier than the Kells Manuscript—belongs to the ninth century, *circa* 830. This would place the Kells volume about the middle of the same century.

The cause of this very wide disagreement is no doubt in the main attributable to the small number of similarly decorated works which are now available for comparison. Brunn is very nearly correct when he states that foliageous ornament is absent in the earlier period of Irish illumination,[2] but he has only the few

1 *Essays and Studies,* 1913.

2 Miss Stokes, too, is quite emphatic in reference to the Book of Durrow, which is admittedly one of the earliest Irish manuscripts: 'There is no sign of any vegetable forms being used.' Yet the illustration she gives from the Book of Durrow (*Early Christian Art in Ireland*, page 17) seems to throw some doubt upon her assertion.

surviving specimens on which to base his judgment. Hundreds of fine manuscripts must have been carried off, burnt, or otherwise destroyed when the Northmen were ravaging Ireland; and it is quite possible that many of those which perished did not conform to Brunn's views as to the absence of phyllomorphic forms. We do know that the Kells Manuscript is full of foliageous forms such as the trefoil and the vine, not to instance others, and that the manuscript which is alone comparable with it in decoration, the Book of Lindisfarne, is practically without them. In the circumstances we must be content to leave the matter in uncertainty, although there is no proof before us that a thorough analytical examination has ever been made by anyone of *all* the manuscripts of the Irish school both at home and abroad.

There is one fact connected with the Book of Kells on which an argument— though not a very strong one— might be founded in support of the later date theory. As previously mentioned, the Manuscript is in a good many of its decorative portions unfinished. It is now certain that some at least of the unfinished ornaments have been continued by an inferior hand. The *Annals of the Four Masters* give us the names of no less than sixty-one remarkable scribes who flourished in Ireland before the year 900, forty of whom lived between A.D. 700 and 800. The art of illumination seems to have deteriorated rapidly in Ireland after about A.D. 900. Now, if the original artist of the Kells Manuscript had almost completed his work at an early date, say between 650 and 750, there would have been roughly a couple of centuries during which the services of one of these 'remarkable scribes' would have been available for the completion of the comparatively small portion left unfinished. Even if originally produced in the year 800, there would have been still one hundred years in which to get a first-class artist to fill the gaps. It is a matter of some difficulty to believe that there *were* such opportunities of completing the volume in a manner worthy of its original condition, and that they were neglected. It is, on the other hand, very easy to see, if the first miniaturist had left his work unfinished, say, late in the ninth century, that there would then have been little chance of procuring the services of an artist equal to the first. The fact that an inferior hand has too frequently left his mark upon the decorations of this splendid manuscript cannot, for the reasons mentioned, do anything to help the cause of those who favour an early date.

One other, now well recognized, method of determining (at least approximately) the date of an early manuscript has not been systematically applied to the Book of Kells. Professor Lindsay and the Palæographical Society have in recent

43

years done excellent work of a general kind in connexion with the subject of contractions in Latin manuscripts, but Ludwig Traube has been the first of our latest commentators to formulate anything in the nature of a law bearing on the date values to be extracted from such shortened forms as are found in early writings. In the case of the word *noster* he has conclusively shown[1] that the forms *nī, no* and *nm* (short for *nostri, nostro,* and *nostrum*) were introduced in the sixth century and predominated in the seventh and eighth; while the forms *nrī, nro,* and *nrm* appear in the eighth century and predominate in the ninth; and it is largely by the application of this law that the New Palæographical Society fix the date of the British Museum manuscript 'Liturgical Prayers' (*Facsimiles,* part VI, plate 132. It is true that the large and bold character of the Kells script does not lend itself much to contraction except in the case of holy words, such as IHS for Jesus, đ for *deus,* sp̄s for *spiritus,* and other usual shortenings; but there are occasional instances of another kind. The letters ae, for example, are now and then abbreviated into ę, a form of contraction that will be found three times on the page set out in plate X and once in plate XV (Mathathie). It is true that this abbreviation occurs in other Irish manuscripts of an early date; but there is a variant of it in the Kells Manuscript which does not seem to have been observed, and one which I have not succeeded in finding elsewhere, viz, â, in which the single-barbed arrow *above* the letter represents the e of the diphthong. It occurs, for instance, in folio 124 verso, where *vae* is written *uâ,* and it will be seen in plate XVI, though in a slightly different position, in connexion with the word *ressa* = ressae. Similarly, in plate XV *ianne* with same mark to right of the e = *iannae.*[2] The fact that this variant is a refinement, as it were, of the other abbreviation of ae, strongly suggests that its use indicates a later date. The matter would seem to be worthy of further palæographical study.

THE ORNAMENTA-TION OF THE ROBES

I have already alluded to a very characteristic form of ornamentation which is found on many of the robes depicted in the Manuscript, or in their immediate neighbourhood in the full-page illuminations, namely the dots, or small circles, in triangular groups. I find no reference to this feature in any of the writings on the Book of Kells, although the consistency with which it manifests itself seems to be full of strong suggestion. If, for obvious reasons, we except the three plates, VIII, XI and XIV, all the full-page illuminations reproduced here will be found to

1 *Nomina Sacra,* Munich, 1907.

2 If it be objected that the arrow in the last two cases is a flourish and not a contraction mark, I would draw attention to the fact that the flourishes here are *attached* to the letter, while contraction marks are *detached.*

44

contain instances of its occurrence. The triangle was, as we know, symbolical of the Trinity, and so of Christianity generally, in medieval times. For this reason perhaps it is that its use in the Book of Kells is confined to the garments, symbols, or surroundings of only holy personages. It is not found, for instance, on the garments of the two Jews in the picture of the arrest of Christ; nor does it appear in connexion with the six small half-figures in the border panel of plate II, all of whom have their backs turned to the Virgin and Child. Its occurrence may therefore be taken to indicate a badge of association with Christ and His teaching: its absence, to denote an anti-Christian attitude, unless there be present some other unmistakable mark of holiness such as wings, book, or blossom-sceptre. I cannot help thinking that an exhaustive investigation of other illuminated manuscripts would produce some new and valuable evidence, arising from the use or the absence of this symbolic ornament, on the question of the date of the Kells Gospels. To what country or school of ornamentation it owes its origin it is at present impossible to say. It does not seem to have been the result of Byzantine influences, for, as a matter of fact, there are no traces of its use in the Book of Lindisfarne, the figure miniatures of which are more Byzantine in their character than those of any other Celtic manuscript. So far as I am aware there is no clear instance of its use in manuscripts of the Irish school at home or abroad before the ninth century; and although it may occasionally be seen in that century in both Celtic and Carolingian illuminations, I have found no such restrictive conditions attaching to its employment as are manifestly observed in its use in the Book of Kells. If this view be undisputed, I can only conclude that we have here yet another fairly reliable proof that the Book of Kells itself cannot have been earlier than the year 800—in other words, that it is a ninth-century manuscript.

The actual writing of the Book of Kells is in itself the embodiment of an early Irish school of calligraphy, which sprang into being in circumstances for which it would be difficult to find a parallel in the history of handwriting in any part of the world. It is acknowledged on all sides that before the arrival of St Patrick in about the year 430, the inhabitants of Ireland were all but destitute of a written literature of any kind. Christianity had undoubtedly made some little way amongst the people before the landing of Patrick, and possibly a few Latin manuscripts may have been used in the service of the earliest missionaries in Ireland. In the written Irish language we have no work surviving, excepting the Book of Armagh, of an earlier date than A.D. 1100.

St Patrick too often has been described as being a single pioneer of Christianity.

He was in reality, as we now know, attended by a large and well-equipped company of earnest workers, carrying with them no small quantity of literary material. If we can accept the Book of Armagh as an authority to be relied on, the missionary party that accompanied St Patrick included some artists. The holy Bishop Assicus was one of them— and is described as Patrick's worker in brass, who was wont to make altars and book-caskets. The same authority tells us that Patrick carried with him to the other side of the Shannon a large number of bells, patens, chalices, altars, law-books and Gospels for use in the churches founded there. Next after his conversion of the Irish Kings, Druids and people, the Saint's greatest achievement was the introduction of the Latin tongue and his making it the ecclesiastical language of Ireland. Tradition tells us, too, that he used himself to write alphabets for young men who were chosen for a clerical career. It is here that his immediate connexion with the Book of Kells becomes apparent; and it is to him, helped by the artistic taste of the schools of Irish penmanship that came after his date, that we are indebted for the striking and always graceful handwriting which is so strong a characteristic of all the early manuscripts of Ireland, and not the least of the Gospels of Colum Cille. The most remarkable feature of this fine type of writing is that, excepting the fact that it developed in Ireland, there is nothing whatever Irish about it. The models employed for the individual letters were purely Roman —the half-uncial forms largely used at the time in Franco-Lombardic and other such manuscripts of Western Europe. But, as Sir Edward M. Thompson tells us[1] 'having once obtained their models, the Irish scribes developed their own style of writing and went on practising it, generation after generation, with astonishing uniformity. The English conquest did not disturb their even course. The invaders concerned themselves not with the language and literature of the country. They were content to use their own style of writing for grants of land and other official deeds; but they left it to the Irish scribes to produce manuscripts in the native characters.'

It is manifest that the high degree of cultivation attained by Irish calligraphy 'did not result,' as Dr F. Keller puts it, 'from the genius of single individuals, but from the emulation of numerous schools of writing, and the improvements of several generations. There is not a single letter in the entire alphabet which does not give evidence, both in its general form and its minuter parts, of the sound judgment and taste of the penman.'[2] In the hand in which the Book of Kells is mainly penned

1 *Greek and Latin Palæography.*
2 *Ulster Journal of Archæology,* VIII, page 223.

46

there are occasional deviations from the standard forms of the Roman half-uncial letters. Two forms of S, for instance, are used, the round capital and the tall half-uncial. A preference is also shown for the capital R—obviously for greater clearness. Three forms of 'a' are used; 'b' and 'l' are always bent; 'd' is shown both with the perpendicular stroke (d) and with the stroke thrown back (δ).[1] Other peculiarities may be noticed in the plates of text.

It may here be mentioned that (as in the case of the illuminations) more than one hand was at work on the script. In addition to the round half-uncial form in which the greater portion of the Book of Kells is written, there are very distinct traces of the handwriting of two other scribes. In one of the folios is an example, as pointed out in the Introduction to Bond and Thomson's *Facsimiles of Manuscripts* (The Palæographical Society, 1873–83). Here the whole page, excepting the last line, 'is transitional, and goes a step nearer to a minuscule form of writing, the letters being thinner in stroke and more compressed; the second, exhibited in the last line, is entirely minuscule, and of the character called pointed. This pointed hand became the ordinary cursive hand of the Irish, which has lasted to the present day.'

The most curious fact connected with the extraordinary adoption by Ireland of the letters of another country is that, although it was at the time merely for the purpose of writing Latin, or the language of the Church, the nation that effected the appropriation has continued from then down to the present to employ, with one or two exceptions, these same Roman letters in the writing of the old Irish language.

The Irish monks not only perfected this script in their native schools, but they carried it with them when any of them left Ireland on their many missions for the propagation of the Christian faith abroad—first to Iona, and from thence to Northumbria, and the South of England, and so on to almost every part of Europe. A very early instance of the effect produced abroad by the Irish is furnished by a manuscript now in St Peter's, Rome: S. Hilarius on the Trinity, the date of which is well established as A.D. 496–523. The writing is described by the editors of the Palæographical Society's *Facsimiles* as 'early minuscule, showing Irish influence . . . the manuscript itself may have been written in Italy, in a monastery where Irish influence was predominant.' Sir Edward M. Thompson acknowledges that England was almost entirely indebted to Ireland for her national handwriting. Miss Stokes, Dr Keller, and others have well described the widespread operations

---

1 Examples of almost all these forms are to be seen in the text reproduced in plate x. See page 33 *ante* for an uncontracted reading of the whole.

of the Irish monks abroad, the monasteries they founded, the libraries they furnished with works of their own hands, written and illuminated in a fashion similar to that of the Book of Kells.

All writers on medieval palæography acknowledge the importance of the Celtic tradition as an influence on the decorative forms of Continental illuminated manuscripts; but it should not be forgotten that the Byzantine school of illumination, with its stern and mosaic-like formality, had been moving steadily westward from very early days in the Christian era. The Book of Lindisfarne, A.D. 800–825, is an instance, with its figures and draperies strongly impressed with traces of Eastern tradition. Italy and France had at an even earlier date been largely affected by the same artistic pressure. The antagonism between the Byzantine and the Celtic ideas of decoration lasted, indeed, for many centuries, each school all the time losing something of its own, and absorbing something in return from the traditions of its opponent. Something approaching a fusion of the two was brought about in a new style of decoration which originated in France under the encouragement of Charlemagne towards the close of the eighth century, and the artistic revival which followed, and spread through western Europe as far as the south of England, may be said to have shaped the spirit and the form of all European pre-Gothic art. Some centuries later the complete interfusion of these clashing traditions resulted in the development of an entirely new type of manuscript illumination both in France and England. Two superb examples of such work, dating from early in the fourteenth century, were presented to the nation within the last two years by Mr H. Yates Thompson, the well-known collector of illuminated manuscripts and books; one of them, the St Omer Psalter, representing the union of the contending schools in their highest state of development in East Anglia, the other, the Metz Pontifical, embodying, though in a less marked degree than the other volume, the amalgamation of Byzantine and Celtic decorative traditions at the top of its perfection in France. Curiously enough, the latter manuscript shares with the Book of Kells the misfortune of having been left unfinished, and the cause of its being so can only be guessed at. Some of its uncompleted pages, however, teach us a good deal as to the actual process of its illumination, a compensation also furnished by the uncompleted portions of the Kells volume. The fuller story of the general influence of the Celtic style of ornament, its spreading, its commingling with decorative forms abroad, and its decline, interesting though it all may be, is outside the purpose of this Introduction.

Returning to the subject of the writing of the Kells Manuscript, we find that

48

differing views have been entertained as to the writing instruments used by the Irish scribes, many palæographers believing that the marked neatness and firmness of the handwriting can only be attributed to the employment of extremely sharp metallic pens or reeds. Amongst the first to reject this belief was Dr Keller, whose opinion—now generally acepted—was that the early Irish pens were the quills of swans, geese, crows, and other birds. The representation of St John in the Book of Kells, plate XVIII, and some other more or less contemporary pictures from ancient manuscripts were rightly relied on by him in support of his contention. The early monkish inkpot is also illustrated in the last-mentioned plate: it was usually conical in shape, and attached either to the arm of the scribe's chair, or fastened to a stick let into the floor. The vellum, or parchment, used by the Irish scribes is generally much thicker than that used by the French from the seventh to the tenth century— the leaves of the Book of Kells are no exception. It is at times finely polished, but more often it is hard and not well cleaned. Goats, sheep, and calves supplied the skins, but the Irish preparation of them was by no means the best.

The blackness of their ancient ink, even at the present, is quite remarkable. It has been found to resist the action of chemical tests of iron, seeming to be composed of materials not generally used in ink making.

In the matter of its punctuation, the written text of the Book of Kells is not a very good example of the Irish practice as described by Dr F. Keller. Speaking of the early Irish manuscripts generally, he tells us that three dots (:·) mark a period; two dots, a comma; (..,) marks a semicolon; and one dot at half the height of the letters, a comma. It is true that instances of the practice may be seen in the present plates and elsewhere in the manuscript, but there does not appear to be anything like the uniformity observed throughout which Dr Keller mentions. The subject, in truth, is one that is only now beginning to be studied with such closeness as is required before we can lay down any really comprehensive rules governing the use of stops by the scribes of early Irish manuscripts. We find, as a fact, in the Book of Kells, many consecutive lines, embracing two or three fully completed sentences, where there is no trace of punctuation at all. The period, or full stop, is variously represented: 1 by three dots (:·); 2 by one dot at half the height of the letter; 3 by omitting the punctuation mark altogether and beginning the next sentence with a striking illuminated initial. So common, indeed, is this last form in the Kells text, that one wonders why full stops should ever be introduced before so obvious an indication of a new sentence as is provided by these fine and constantly recurring initials. Occasionally also the very size of the initial tells a reader the value of the stop—as, for instance, where a half-height dot is followed by a small initial, one knows it is something in the nature of a comma. The half-height dot is also used to mark the commencement of a speech, as a colon is commonly used to-day.

Another point connected with the punctuation found in the Kells Manuscript has, so far as I am aware, been overlooked by all palæographers. None of them seems to have noticed that the dots of which the punctuation is formed are, in the Kells volume, almost always square in shape, or quadrilateral—not round. In itself it would seem to be a matter of little moment; and one might easily jump to the conclusion that this particular shape was employed as best suited to fit in with the type of letters used. There may, however, be a deeper meaning attached to it, and one possibly capable of throwing some light on the question of the date of the Manuscript. A cursory examination of such reproductions of Latin script as are set out in Sir Edward M. Thompson's admirable book, *Greek and Latin Palæography*, the *Facsimiles* of the Palæographical Society, and some other works of a similar nature that I have consulted, shows with considerable clearness that the square form of punctuation marks does not seem to have been common until about the tenth century. Traces of its use are no doubt to be met with in one or two manuscripts supposed to be of an earlier date; but there will, I think, be found after the tenth century and on to the twelfth a very striking consistency in the use of square, and not round, punctuation. In no other manuscript or reproduction that I have seen are there such clear-cut, square-shaped stops as in the Book of Kells. I would suggest, though with much diffidence, that as in the case of musical notation, where the earlier square form gave place, at a more or less definite date, to the round form now almost universally made use of, so here may perhaps be found an additional argument for ascribing a later date to the Book of Kells than that assumed by the majority of students.

THE ORNAMENTA- TION OF THE MANUSCRIPT The ornamentation of the Book of Kells when broken up into its component parts will be found to be made up of four main divisions. The same, if we except phyllo-morphic forms, may be said of nearly all the other decorated manuscripts produced in or about the same period:

1 Patterns in the composition of which geometrical combinations or develop-ments of straight or curved lines form the sole element, viz, the spiral and the interlacing.
2 Zoomorphic, or animal forms.

3 Phyllomorphic, or leaf and plant forms: the two last-named classes being motives of a conventionalized kind, which though unnatural in treatment are derived from nature.

4 Figure representations.

A good deal has been written on the three less important divisions of decorative types—I shall return to them later—but of infinitely greater interest are the subdivisions of the first class which embody all that can be described as Celtic art in its most characteristic expressions, the spiral and the interlacement—and which, singly or in combination, are woven with such unerring taste into the decorative texture of the Book of Kells. With the origin of these is involved the story of prehistoric national art tendencies which go back into the mists of long-forgotten ages. Their very existence in far-away times can only be surmised; their developments can only be extracted as it were by a process of spectrum analysis from the converging rays of a remote antiquity which are gathered into focus in the illumination of such a volume as the Gospels of Colum Cille and other works of a similarly decorative type. In truth, underlying these two apparently simple forms of design is a racial romance, which commences with the earliest origin of the Indo-European immigration, and continues through thousands of years, and in ever-shifting changes of scene, down to the time at which the westward-tending multitudes began to settle in Ireland and form what has since been known as the early Irish people.

The trumpet pattern, or divergent spiral, as will be seen in many of the plates, is composed of two winding lines which afterwards diverge into a trumpet form, the open end of which is closed by a curved line. A new spiral springs in inverted order from the points of the curved line—the two winding lines repeating the original pattern in converging directions until they reach a central point. Then they start again, diverging and converging as before in an almost infinite succession of spiral forms. In its earliest type, as found in the great tumuli of the New Grange Group, *circa* 1200 B.C. and later between 200 B.C. and A.D. 200 on metal ornaments, the curve is large and simple; in Christian times the curved spaces were treated as secondary to the spiral and the turns round the central point are frequently twelve or more. After the tenth, and perhaps the beginning of the eleventh century, this design seems to have dropped out of Irish art. As a form of simple decoration its origin is possibly coeval with the earliest efforts of the most archaic civilization. In pre-Hellenic ages, about 2200 B.C. it was already well known in Crete, as shown by the Kamares vases found within the last fourteen years in the now excavated

Palace of Phaestos. From thence it passed to Egypt and Mycenæ. The wandering races, whether Tuatha da Danaan, Firbolgs, Celts, or Milesians that ultimately reached and settled in Ireland, had, on their way west from Scythia and the Ægean, been in touch with many forms of civilization. Those of them that took the South European route dwelt long in Egypt, Greece, Crete, Italy, and Spain; those that took a more northerly and transalpine way had, under the name of Celtæ, occupied all central Gaul; while others of them spread through north-west Europe, making their chief seat in Scandinavia. Each succeeding wave brought its own types of ornament, tribal or national as the case might be, changed perhaps in trivial respects from what they were originally, but sufficiently characteristic to form the basis of higher artistic developments when occasion arose for putting them to use.[1]

In the words of Johan A. Brunn,[2] whose name I have already mentioned: 'The spiral design was no accidental feature in the pages of Celtic art, nor was it confined to such simple, uniform scrolls as those we find used as a kind of border ornament by several prehistoric peoples. It was, on the contrary, a favourite pattern of a very elaborate character, applied as a surface decoration to a variety of objects, such as shields, helmets, sword sheaths, armlets, horse-trappings, and personal ornaments, examples of which still survive, testifying to an astonishing proficiency in metal work—bronze and gold—both as regards construction and decoration.

'It has been suggested that, at least in some types, it was developed under the influence of floral or foliated schemes transplanted from classical ground.[3] If so, that might account for part of its force and freedom, qualities so rare in an ornament of purely geometrical extraction; while, on the other hand, in case the opinion be correct, the Celtic pattern may be said to be the most ingenious translation ever made of a foliageous design into a geometrical one. One might think of its being introduced together with the stock of ornaments brought from other

1 Mr George Coffey (*The Bronze Age in Ireland*, 1913) writes: 'Ireland during the Bronze Age was not isolated, but stood in direct communication with the Continent. Ægean and Scandinavian influences can be detected in the great tumuli of the New Grange Group, and Iberian influence is discernible in some of the later types of bronze implements. Ireland . . . was during the Bronze Age a kind of western El Dorado, owing to her great richness in gold.' Mr Coffey assumes that spirals were introduced from Scandinavia, where this motive had penetrated early from the Ægean along the amber route.

2 *An Enquiry into the Art of the Illuminated MSS. of the Middle Ages, op. cit.*

3 Mr George Coffey, for instance, thinks that Celtic designs were (after 400 B.C.) influenced by classical anthemion and meander patterns, which were modified by the Celtic love of spiral and scroll.

52

countries by the early Christian missionaries. But it would be very difficult, if not impossible, to point to a single scheme in decorative art outside of the Celtic area with greater claim than the so-called late Celtic to be considered as the prototype that suggested the spiral design shown in manuscripts and other works of the Christian era.'

The second subdivision of the main or first-class type, the interlacement pattern, is also well described by Brunn:

INTER-
LACING

'This type of pattern may be characterized as a surface decoration composed of one or more ribbons or straps of uniform size, which are twisted, plaited, knotted, or otherwise interwoven so as to cover the field with a symmetrically disposed design. It occurs in a variety of forms, from the plain twist, or guilloche, to the elaborate chain composed of knots of torturing intricacy and of varied construction, being laid in squares, circles, oblongs, triangles, hexagons, octagons, etc. The more intricate forms are predominant; and, by variety of design and the unerring precision with which the ribbons are interwoven so as to cross over and under alternately and finally be joined up to each other, testify to the astonishing capacity of the draughtsman. When compared with the spiral ornament, the interlaced work looks rather mechanical . . . Hence it came that these held a very subordinate place to the more complicated patterns. An interlaced series would receive an additional enrichment in various ways.'

The immediate origin of this universally characteristic feature of Celtic illumination is in all probability to be found in decorative remains of North Italy and Southern Gaul dating from the second and third centuries. It did not become widely popular in Irish art until the seventh century.

Amongst other geometrical motives of which the first division is composed, should be included the fret pattern, which is employed in a considerable number or forms as a filling for panels in both borders and initials. The peculiarity of the Celtic fret, which is strongly distinguished from the square type so usual in Greek art, lies in the bending of the links, at certain points, at angles of 45 degrees instead of 90 degrees. The whole assumes in this way a peculiar Chinese character.

FRET AND
DIAPER
PATTERNS

Diaper work is occasionally introduced to brighten small spaces lying between the larger designs of more extended elaboration. It occurs in the Book of Kells in many varieties, and in conjunction with rosettes, a detail of ornamentation somewhat foreign to Celtic art.

Dots, too, mostly red in colour, are one of the leading features of the less important details of decoration. They are often used by themselves to form patterns

DOTTED
PATTERNS

in extended lines for filling vacant spaces in a large design, as in the Book of Lindisfarne. Their more usual employment in the Book of Kells is for the purpose of adding as it were a fringe to exterior lines. Their use is very frequently relied on in the case of the smaller initials (see plates XX–XXIV).

A somewhat curious distinction, in relation to this type of ornamentation, is to be found between the Book of Kells and the Lindisfarne Gospels. In the former the dots are almost always in single lines, while in the latter they are frequently used in double lines, producing a somewhat richer form of fringe.[1]

PLANT FORMS OF DECORATION In the matter of phyllomorphic forms the decoration of the Book of Kells presents a remarkable contrast to nearly all the early Irish illuminated manuscripts. J. A. Brunn goes so far as to say: 'Foliageous ornament is entirely unknown in the Celtic illuminated manuscripts of the earlier period.' The presence of these forms here will be obvious to any observer of the details of the plates reproduced in this volume. Their introduction is in many respects, however, extremely difficult to account for. Brunn has well described what he styles this 'most important innovation,' but without drawing any definite conclusion as to the exact meaning of its first appearance in this manuscript:

'The element appears, to begin with, among the flourishes and terminals, in the shape of lightly sketched branches with leaves and flowers, sometimes proceeding from vases. Of a more elaborate nature are the scrolls of foliage which are seen to fill in, as a surface decoration, long, narrow borders or panels in the grand illuminated pages. The most characteristic form is a pattern of a single wavy stem with alternate recurved scrolls terminating in trefoil-shaped leaves. Also in this position the stem is occasionally found to proceed from a vase. More general, however, is a less rational connexion of leaf design with zoomorphic patterns. Thus a branch of foliage is frequently seen to evolve from between the open jaws of a nondescript, while at the same time the tail of the beast presents the appearance of a trefoil or lance-shaped leaf. And there are other patterns in which zoomorphic forms are intertwined with undulating stems of foliage, much on the same principle as the compositions which, in the previous pages, we have observed in dialects of non-Celtic decorative art.'

The fact stated by Brunn, like all statements of fact regarding the Irish illuminations, is, of course, based only on the evidence supplied by the still surviving examples of such work. It is, no doubt, within the bounds of possibility that some strange

---

1 The double rows of red dots are also found in MacDurnan's Gospels (Lambeth Palace Library), but this manuscript is not regarded as earlier than the end of the ninth century.

and accidental recovery of other examples of the many manuscripts which have disappeared long ago might upset any theories formed on the decorative features of those which we actually possess; but until such recovery be made it seems rational to assume that the subsisting specimens represent the average character of those which have perished. But here is the difficulty if we act on this assumption. The majority of palæographers put the date of the Book of Kells as not later than the eighth century. Do any of this majority allow that leaf or plant forms of decoration are found so early in other existing Celtic manuscripts? If not, the Kells manuscript, although confessed by all to have reached the high-level mark in Irish illumination, occupies a strangely isolated position in the Celtic schools of decoration, where it never inspired even a single scribe to imitate in other works the effects produced by its artistic introduction of new foliageous forms. If, on the other hand, the date of the Kells Gospels be brought down to the ninth century or later, the innovation of its leaf and plant ornamentation ceases to be striking, and fits in with what most critics allow to be the case; as well as smoothing over some other incongruities (already referred to) which are inseparable from any theory of an earlier production.

No account that might be written of the zoomorphic, or animal, forms introduced in the decoration of the manuscript could convey any impression of a more effective kind than that given by the plates themselves. At the same time it is well to bear in mind that the true explanation of their unnatural drawing is not to be attributed to the incapacity of the artist. Such deviations from nature as they exhibit are due more or less to the same causes that led to the eccentricities attaching to the human figures represented: in other words, there never was any intention on the artist's part to depict these animal forms in their natural shapes. Whatever they happen to be, fish, peacock, horse, dog, hare, otter, cat, rat, cock, lizard, serpent, or dragon, they are all in a sense creatures of a world apart, strongly marked with the deliberate unreality of ecclesiastical heraldry; distant relations, as it were, of the lion, the calf, and the eagle, of the Evangelical symbols, and forced into disnatured anatomies and fantastic posturings only to serve the purposes of the artist, and fall in with the general decorative scheme of which they form a symmetrical part. In this way only, according to the tenets of the early Irish School of illumination, could artistic harmony be preserved; and curious as such living forms may be when contrasted with the more correct and altogether natural pictures of animal life in the Continental manuscripts of a later day, it can at least be said that, as compared with the strange creatures we have been long familiar with in heraldry, the fauna of the Book of Kells are not much more extravagant than the singular creatures that owe their origin to the Heralds' College.

SERPENTINE
DECORATION

The frequently recurring presence of serpentine forms all through the decorations of the manuscript has given rise to the suggestion that these forms are in some way connected with the worship of ophidian reptiles. There certainly appears to be some evidence to show that amongst the immigrant races that had established themselves in the land before the introduction of Christianity the worship of the serpent was practised, though perhaps not very widely. It is even possible that this was the serpent which St Patrick is said to have driven out of the country. The adoption of this serpentine form by the Church for decorative purposes would have been but another instance of what we know was the custom of the Christian Church in very early days, when many pagan elements were for good reasons absorbed into the practices of the Christian missionaries, and afterwards became permanently interwoven with Christian belief. Both St Jerome and St Augustine strongly upheld this course of action on grounds of expediency when dealing with converts from paganism.

Dr F. Keller, writing of Irish early ornament generally, says: 'In all these ornaments there breathes a peculiar spirit, which is foreign to the people of the West: there is in them a something mysterious which imparts to the eye a certain feeling of uneasiness and suspense. This is especially the case with those frightful-looking monstrous figures of animals, whose limbs twist and twine themselves into a labyrinth of ornaments, where one can hardly resist the natural impulse to search for the other parts of their bodies, often nearly concealed or passing into different strange creatures . . . The variety of these forms . . . their luxuriant development, often extravagant, but sometimes uncommonly delicate and lovely . . . must have been originated in the East, or at least have their prototypes there. That the Irish system of ornamentation does actually find an analogy in Eastern countries is proved by the illustrations published by C. Knight in a small work on Egypt. We find there the serpentine bands of the Irish ornaments appearing already in the oldest Egyptian and Ethiopian manuscripts, and with a similarity of colour and combination truly astonishing.'

THE
FIGURES
OF THE
MANUSCRIPT

When we come to consider the fourth division of the ornamentation of the manuscript, it may be said that, among the many strange features of this remarkable volume, there is none stranger than the representation it gives us of the human figure. Such adjectives as 'barbaric,' 'grotesque,' 'distressing,' 'hideous,' with others of a like kind, are commonly used by writers when referring to them; and suggestions are boldly put forward to the effect that in spite of all their capability for decoration of the highest kind, the hands that framed, and the minds that conceived the ornamental pages of this very marvellous work were unable to present either human or superhuman faces, their anatomy, or their garments, in any other but the apparently inadequate form in which such drawings have been made. Ruskin's words[1] on this subject are: 'The Celts developing peculiar gifts in linear design, but wholly incapable of drawing animals or figures'—a comment based upon an obviously superficial knowledge of the aims of the Irish illuminators. Byzantine influences are strongly relied on by some high authorities as being the controlling lead that shaped their eccentricities, and even relied on by such of them as deny the possibility of Byzantium having had anything to do with the purely ornamental accessories which surround these very figure drawings. That extremely intelligent writer on Celtic illumination, Johan A. Brunn,[2] expresses his views on the subject thus:

'It may be that this very imperfect style of draughtsmanship, which appears to modern onlookers so ridiculously childish and grotesque, was viewed by its contemporaries with a very different eye from that with which a modern critic views the same thing. It may be that the absurdities in form and colour, which make the figures of the Saviour and His Apostles appear to us like so many rudely expressed travesties, were veiled by a sentiment similar to that which makes the pious Catholic of our days kneel down to the image of the Crucified, quite unheeding whether it be the beautifully finished work of a world-known artist or the badly carved and badly painted puppet from the workshop of some rustic *Herrgott-Schnitzer*; it may be that the devotional fervour with which everything connected with religion was approached by the faithful of the day cast around the illustrative efforts of the school a halo of sanctity which made their absurdities disappear to a sympathizing and uncritical onlooker . . . The same conventionalizing tendencies as were shown in the treatment of the pure ornament reappear in the drawing and colouring of the human figure . . . In moulding the type of the head the ever-present spiral was resorted to as a capital means of putting the face into the requisite shape, by regulating the troublesome curves of the nose, the mouth and the ears.[3]

1 *The Pleasures of England.*

2 *An Enquiry into the Art of the Illuminated MSS. of the Middle Ages, op. cit.*

3 A singular example of this artistic coercion will be seen in plate xviii, where the top edge of a book is *rounded* so as to be in proper alignment with the nimbus upon which it impinges.

This undoubtedly added to the regularity of the type, but unfortunately not to its beauty.'

Again, in reference to animal forms, and the conventionalizing of them, the same author writes: 'Here it is, if possible, even more conspicuous. The spiral recurs in the ears, jaws, and junction of the limbs with the body. The whole space of the body is frequently covered with an intricate pattern of some of the ordinary types, and the colours are distributed without the slightest regard to nature.'

Again, speaking of Celtic illuminations generally, he says: 'And yet they are not so utterly destitute of all artistic merit as some people think. . . . And there are miniature pages, as, for example, in the Book of Kells, where the odd formulæ in which the figures appear are in such singular harmony with the innermost character of the ornaments, and the two elements, miniature and ornament, are so admirably united with a consistent whole of most original aspect, that we are well justified in speaking of a style with reference to similar productions. It might be supposed that a school characterized by the intense Celticism of these and similar productions owed little or nothing to the art of miniature painting as cultivated outside of the Celtic area. Yet this is not the case.'

Brunn goes on to show that such paintings are ultimately traceable to non-Celtic models—in other words, to Byzantine or Italo-Byzantine illuminated manuscripts of contemporary or still remoter date: 'How this was brought about has yet to be shown.'

HERALDIC FORM
A much simpler explanation would seem to be that all the apparently weird figures of either Saviour, saint or man which meet us in the pages of the Book of Kells, not to mention other manuscripts of about the same period, are, in reality, what might now be termed heraldic. Their being so gives them at once an artistic as well as a theological value. They are heraldic because no other form of pictorially personified humanity could be made to fit in with the decorative surroundings in which they are enshrined; while the deliberate avoidance of any real resemblance to humanity only intensifies the spirit of reverence for holy things possessed by the illuminators. Independently of such reasons, however, it should not be forgotten that the Eastern Church had from an early date laid down very definite instructions in reference to the representation of holy personages; and undoubtedly such instructions in a pictorial form had reached Ireland from Italy and southern France at the periods when her school of illumination was in its incipient and its progressive state. These Eastern instructions were long afterwards collected into a book called *The Painter's Guide*, which was compiled at Mount Athos, in Greece,

58

from the works of Pauselinos, a painter of the eleventh century, a volume which ultimately became the text-book of Byzantine art. In a like way the Irish 'Book of Ballymote', A.D. 1300, prescribed the formalities with which the Apostles and other holy personages should be painted; and there are points in common between the teaching of the two works, as Miss Margaret Stokes has pointed out in her very interesting reference to this subject, though the two manuals are by no means unanimous all through.[1] For example (amongst many that might be mentioned), in the case of the representation of St John the Evangelist, the Eastern practice was to paint him as 'an old man, bald, large, not very thick beard'; while the Irish painters were enjoined by both the Book of Ballymote and by the ancient Irish poem in the Codex Maelbrighte to depict him 'without any beard.'[2]

Celtic departures from the formalities prescribed by Eastern authority— and they are frequent— would seem to point to the existence of an early traditional treatment of such matters in Ireland which had been followed for perhaps some centuries before the appearance of the Byzantine *Painter's Guide*. It is certainly easier to think that the portrait figures of the Book of Kells and similar Irish manuscripts were the direct result of some such local tradition than to assume that the gifted illuminators of the marvellously drawn decorative portions of such works were unable to paint the human form, had they wished to do so, in a more natural way than they have done.

The smaller illuminated initials, which, owing to their great profusion, would distinguish the Book of Kells from every other manuscript ever written, are reproduced here in a goodly number. Some idea of the total number of these very exquisite gems may be gathered from the fact that, excluding the large illuminations, every verse of every chapter in the four Gospels commences with one of them. Their infinite variety shows an artistic originality of a perfectly bewildering nature. Their beauty of form and colour is reproduced with a rare fidelity in our illustrations, plates XX to XXIV which are taken from the copies made by the late Mrs Helen Campbell d'Olier, of Dublin, a highly gifted illuminator who devoted a great portion of her life to the work. There are no two of these letters the same throughout the whole volume; and even the compound letters of the

THE
SMALLER
ILLUMINA-
TIONS

1 *Early Christian Art in Ireland.*

2 It is worthy of notice that St John in the Kells Manuscript has fair hair *and* a beard, while the St John of the Book of Lindisfarne has no beard. The latter deviation is the more remarkable as the Lindisfarne portraits are generally assumed to be more Byzantine than those in the Book of Kells.

word ET which occur so very many times, never appear twice in the same form. Many of the originals are exhibited in the Library of Trinity College, Dublin.

The subject of the actual pigments used in the general decoration of the Book of Kells is one of considerable interest; but it is only from comparatively recent investigations that any information has been acquired in connexion with this obscure branch of Irish palæography. There is as yet no absolute certainty as to either the colours used, or the wonderful durability attaching to them, but microscopic examination has succeeded in rescuing some at least of the materials from oblivion. Professor Hartley, who has gone into the matter more thoroughly than others, gives his conclusions in a paper published in the Proceedings of the Royal Dublin Society, N.S. volume IV, 1885: 'A very careful examination of the work shows that the pigments mixed with gum, glue, or gelatine are laid on somewhat thickly—there is no staining of the vellum and no mingling of tints. There is, however, as was pointed out to me, a painting of blue over a ground of green.'

His conclusions as to the materials of which the colours are compounded are briefly as follows: The black is lamp black, or possibly fish-bone black; the bright red is realgar (arsenic disulphide, As_2S_2); the yellow, orpiment (arsenic tersulphide, As_2S_3); the emerald green, malachite; the deep blue, possibly lapis lazuli, but owing to its transparency when overlying green, more likely not so. The reddish-purple is, he thinks, either a finely ground glass coloured with gold, or a preparation like 'the purple of Cassius,' which is obtained from a solution of gold by the action of a solution of tin, and was extremely costly. It is used very sparingly in the Kells Manuscript, a fact that confirms his view. The other colours used are neutral green, a tint resembling burnt sienna, a pale blue and lilac. Professor Hartley concludes his paper thus:

'The master who taught the art of designing and painting to the artist who executed the Book of Kells unquestionably knew how to prepare the colours. As for the materials, malachite . . . green in colour, is found near Cork and Limerick; chrysocolla . . . green to blue in colour, is found in the County Cork; chrome, hæmatite, and ochres occur in the County Wicklow; of red hæmatite of an earthy nature, such as is termed raddle, there is a plentiful supply in the County Antrim. Orpiment and realgar must have been obtained from elsewhere, and the purples were undoubtedly of artificial origin; it is probable they were brought from abroad, and such colours were no doubt treasured as jewels.'

It remains for me to express my regret at the loss which Trinity College, Dublin, has suffered by the death in 1913 of its late librarian, the Rev Dr Abbott, whose scholarly collation of the Book of Kells and other early Irish texts is well known to all students of biblical history. My best thanks are due to Mr Alfred de Burgh, the sub-librarian, for his courteous assistance and valuable suggestions during my study of the manuscript.

EDWARD SULLIVAN 1914

THE PLATES

PLATE I

folio 5 recto. A page of the Eusebian Canons

see text page 24

PLATE II

folio 7 verso. The Virgin and Child

see text page 24

PLATE III

folio 19 verso. Portion of the 'Argument' to the Gospel of St John

see text pages 23 and 26

exponicur uescienoi desiderio collocacio **G**

quicerenubus fruccus laboris et do magiste

rii doccrina serueccur—

ricce sacerdoci appa

ruic angelus et adnunciauic ei filium Ioha=

nnen **G** idem mariae adnunciauic angelus

filium ihm **C** toribus ∴ **G** acca

N acauicacem ihu adnunciac angelus pas

pic simeon puerum ihin **G** benedixic

din et anna profecassa bac

G anorum duodecim ihs incemplo doce

seniores asmum poenicec

U bi iohannis bapcazac populum bap

PLATE IV

folio 27 verso. The Evangelical Symbols

see text pages 27 and 35

PLATE V

folio 28 verso. Portrait of St Matthew

see text pages 27, 29 and 30

PLATE VI

folio 29 recto. The opening words of St Matthew's gospel

LIBER

GENE

RATI

ONIS

see text pages 27, 28, 34 and 37

PLATE VII

folio 32 verso. Portrait of St Mark or St Luke

see text pages 28, 29 and 30

PLATE VIII

folio 33 recto. The Eight-circled Cross

see text page 30

PLATE IX

folio 34 recto. The Monogram Page

XPI B. GENERATIO

Christi autem generatio
MATTHEW i. 18

see text pages 31 and 34

hgeneratio

Ae autem praegnantibus &

nutrientibus in illis diebus :⁘

Orate autem ut non fiat fuga

uestra hieme uel sabbato :⁘

Erit enim tunc tribulatio magna

qualis non fuit ab initio mun

di usque modo neque fiet :⁘

Et nisi breuiata fuissent dies

illi non fieret salua om

nis caro sed propter electos bre

uiabuntur dies illi :⁘

Tunc siquis uobis dixerit ecce

hic xps aut illic nolite credere

Rtent enim pseudo xpi &

pseudo profetae & dabunt

signa magna & prodigia ita in erro

rem inducantur si fieri potest etiam

PLATE X

folio 104 recto. A page of the text

MATTHEW xxiv. 19–24

see text pages 23 and 32

PLATE XI

folio 124 recto. *Tunc crucifixerant XPI cum eo duos latrones*

TUNC CRU

CIFIXERANT

XPI CUM EO DU

OS LATRONES

MATTHEW XXVii. 38

see text pages 33 and 35

PLATE XII

folio 129 verso. The Evangelical Symbols

see text pages 34 *and* 35

PLATE XIII

folio 130 recto. The opening words of St Mark's Gospel

INI TI UM

EVAN GE

LII IHU

XPI

Initium evangelii Ihu Xpi

see text pages 34 and 35

PLATE XIV

folio 188 recto. The opening word of St Luke's Gospel

QUON

IAM

quoniam

see text page 35

PLATE XV

folio 200 recto. The Genealogy of Christ

FACTA EST TU ES FILIUS MEUS DILECTUS IN TE

BENE CONPLACUIT MIHI

ET IPSE IHS ERAT INCIPIENS QUASI AN

NORUM TRIGINTA UT PUTABATUR FILIUS

IOSEPH

    QUI FUIT HELI

    QUI FUIT MATHA

    QUI FUIT LEVI

    QUI FUIT MELCHI

    QUI FUIT IANNAE

    QUI FUIT IOSEPH

    QUI FUIT MATHATHIE

    QUI FUIT AMOS

    QUI FUIT NAUUM

    QUI FUIT ESLI

    QUI FUIT NAGGE

    QUI FUIT MAATH

        LUKE iii. 22–6

see text pages 35 and 36

facttt est tu es filius meus dilectus in te

bene—conplacuit mihi

Et ipse ihs erat incipiens quasi an

norum triginta ut putabatur filius

Ioseph

VI · fuit · heli

VI · fuit · matha

VI · fuit · leui

VI · fuit · melchi

VI · fuit · iannae

VI · fuit · ioseph

VI · fuit · mathat hic

VI · fuit · amos

VI · fuit · naum

VI · fuit · esli

VI · fuit · nagge

VI · fuit · maath

ui	fuit	enachath
ui	fuit	iate
ui	fuit	semei
ui	fuit	ioseph osse
ui	fuit	iuda
ui	fuit	iohanna
ui	fuit	ressa
ui	fuit	zorbba
ui	fuit	salachiel
ui	fuit	·ieri
ui	fuit	melchi
ui	fuit	addi
ui	fuit	cosan
ui	fuit	elmadam
ui	fuit	er
ui	fuit	iesu
ui	fuit	eliezer

PLATE XVI

folio 200 verso. The Genealogy of Christ: *continued*

QUI FUIT MATHATH

QUI FUIT IAE

QUI FUIT SYMEI

QUI FUIT IOSEPH. OSSE

QUI FUIT IUDA

QUI FUIT JOHANNA

QUI FUIT RESSAE

QUI FUIT ZORBBA

QUI FUIT SALATHIEL

QUI FUIT NERI

QUI FUIT MELCHI

QUI FUIT ADDI

QUI FUIT COSAM

QUI FUIT ELMADAM

QUI FUIT ER

QUI FUIT IESU

QUI FUIT ELIEZER

N.B.   The two first lines are an uncorrected error. They should read:
qui fuit mathathiae—omitting the second *qui fuit*

PLATE XVII

folio 201 recto. The Genealogy of Christ: *continued*

QUI FUIT ZORIM

QUI FUIT MATHAT

QUI FUIT LEVI

QUI FUIT SEMEON

QUI FUIT IUDA

QUI FUIT JOSEPH

QUI FUIT IONA

QUI FUIT ELIACIM

QUI FUIT MELCHA

QUI FUIT MENNA

QUI FUIT MATHATHIA

QUI FUIT NATHAN

QUI FUIT DAVID

QUI FUIT IESSE

QUI FUIT OBED

QUI FUIT BOOS

QUI FUIT SALMON

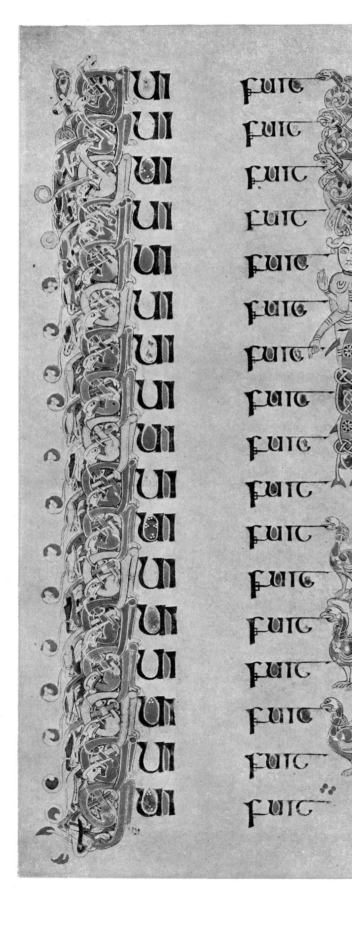

fuit zorim
fuit macchat
fuit leui
fuit semeon
fuit iuda
fuit ioseph
fuit iona
fuit eliacim
fuit melcha
fuit menna
fuit macchathia
fuit nathan
fuit dauid
fuit iesse
fuit obed
fuit boos
fuit salmon

PLATE XVIII

folio 291 verso. Portrait of St John

This is one of the pages which have suffered most at the hands of the binder about
140 years ago (see page vi).

see text pages 29, 37 and 49

PLATE XIX

folio 292 recto. The opening words of St John's Gospel

IN P

RINCI

PIOERAT VER

BUMETVERBUM

In principio erat Verbum et Verbum

see text pages 34 *and* 37

PLATE XX

Compound letters *from copies by Helen Campbell d'Olier.*

Q	R	Q
	ET	
AD (tendite)	AD	AI AT i (lli)

PLATE XXI

Compound letters *from copies by Helen Campbell d'Olier.*

AV	ET DIXit	PO (nite)
Pa(ter) A (pparuit)	ID AS	B(eati) B ,, B ,, B ,, B ,,

PLATE XXII

Compound letters *from copies by Helen Campbell d'Olier.*

Bonum	Ecce	TRadat
Cum ergo	Illis	S
Vesper	Haec	DIco

PLATE XXIII

Compound letters *from copies by Helen Campbell d'Olier.*

QUi dixit	GEneratio
DIXerunt	SEd neque

Ui dixit

Neravo

Xerunt

Cliteque

Iicet panis

uicc

Ropter

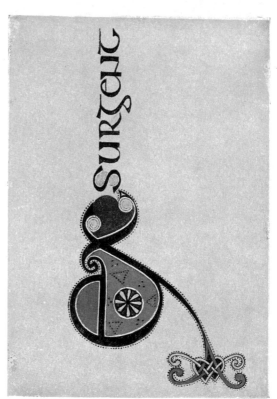

Surgent

PLATE XXIV

Compound letters *from copies by Helen Campbell d'Olier.*

HIc est panis	CAvete
PRopter	EXsurgent